*And the effect of righteousness will be peace, and the
result of righteousness, quietness and trust for ever.*

Isaiah 32:17

*They have healed the wound of my people lightly, saying,
"Peace, peace," when there is no peace.*

Jeremiah 6:14; 8:11

*"It seems to depend on nothing but the ill-humour of Mrs.
Churchill, which I imagine to be the most certain thing in
the world." "My Emma!" replied Mrs. Weston, smiling,
"what is the certainty of caprice?"*

Jane Austen, *Emma*

PEACE AND CERTAINTY

A THEOLOGICAL ESSAY ON DETERRENCE

Oliver O'Donovan

WILLIAM B. EERDMANS PUBLISHING COMPANY
GRAND RAPIDS, MICHIGAN

Copyright © 1989 Oliver O'Donovan

First published 1989 by Wm. B. Eerdmans Publishing Company
255 Jefferson Ave. S.E., Grand Rapids, Michigan 49503

Library of Congress Cataloging-in-Publication Data

O'Donovan, Oliver.
Peace and certainty: a theological essay on deterrence /
Oliver O'Donovan
p.   cm.
ISBN 0-8028-0414-4
1. Deterrence (Strategy)—Religious aspects—Christianity.
2. Nuclear warfare—Religious aspects—Christianity.
3. Deterrence (Strategy)—moral and ethical aspects.
4. Nuclear warfare—Moral and ethical aspects.
I. Title.
U162.6.O53   1988
261.8'73—dc19   88-25929
CIP

Contents

Acknowledgments   *vii*

CHAPTER I
Scope   *1*

CHAPTER II
Growth   *31*

CHAPTER III
Failure   *55*

CHAPTER IV
Intention   *77*

CHAPTER V
Peacemaking   *99*

Acknowledgments

THIS theological essay on deterrence began life while its author was a very well treated guest of the University of Durham in February 1987, delivering the annual lectures in Pastoral Theology which are held under the auspices of the Department of Theology and the theological colleges. My hosts graciously permitted me to use the occasion to speak on a theme which does not fall within the usually accepted purview of "pastoral" theology, and gave me a stimulating reception. It has since benefited from the kindness of my colleague Professor Rowan Williams and of the Bishop of Oxford, the Rt. Rev. Richard Harries, who have criticised it in draft and provoked me to undertake considerable revision. I was also much assisted by a brief visit to NATO in Brussels made possible by the British North Atlantic Committee, and remember with appreciation the frankness and geniality with which members of the NATO staff and of the British and American delegations opened themselves to discussion of the important issues. Needless to say, my views are my own.

I must mention a debt of another kind, which will be evident anyway to the reader between the lines, but will bear confessing. That is to Paul Ramsey, who died while this book was on its journey from the author to the public. His writings on war and deterrence from the sixties provide both the starting point and the measure of intellectual seriousness for all Christian discussion since. The re-reading of his classic writings has forced me to review my positions and face new questions more effectively than any recent contribution to the literature, excellent as some of these have been. Professor Ramsey's last kindness to me was to permit me an advance view of his book *Speak Up for Just War or Pacifism*, since published posthumously.

The composition of this little essay began, as readers with an eye for chronology will note, in the dark days of the debacle at Reykjavik, and reached its final stages more or less contemporaneously with the signing of the intermediate-range weapons treaty. This welcome event—for who could be so sour as to refuse the happy omen for East-West relations?—impressed the general public, or that part of it which concerns itself with grave questions of principle, with the comfortable conviction that the problem of deterrence was now solved, so that the question disappeared from public debate, inside and outside the churches, almost as suddenly as it did at the time of the brief cold-war thaw in the early seventies. But the treaty has resolved nothing at the level of principle. Viewed in the context of the deterrent forces that remain, indeed, it represents nothing but a swing of the deterrence-pendulum back from "flexible" to "massive" retaliation. This is my excuse, not only for troubling the public further on a question that is thought to be settled, but for devoting little notice in my discussion to the treaty itself.

A friendly member of the audience at Durham remarked brightly after the third of four lectures: "Well, tomorrow I expect we shall get to the theology!" To those who share his bewilderment at the distance moral theology must sometimes travel from its exegetical and credal base-camp, it may be some comfort to be told that the tensions this generates are felt as strongly by those who journey as by those who wait for their return. I would like to think that a reader who is acquainted with other work of mine will be prepared to take it on trust that I have not forgotten where the theologian's starting-point must be, even if, in a "dialectic" essay such as this, I have not made the whole route out and back quite explicit. But (not to presume upon that trust too far) I am perfectly aware that a really thorough "analytic" of political theology is a major intellectual lack of our time. In an ideally-ordered field of study, a Germanic science such as Prince Andrei would loathe, we would establish our right and our method first. But in circumstances of pressing pastoral urgency (for deterrence is, after all, a pastoral concern in the widest sense) we cannot wait to do things in order, but must proclaim the Gospel directly into the situation that confronts us. If we do indeed speak in words taught by the Spirit, we may presume upon the comparing of spiritual things with spiritual.

Christ Church, Oxford.

CHAPTER I

Scope

DETERRENCE is the name we have given to the stance of perpetual armed threat with which the two great political blocs of the post-war world confront each other. That is the theme of these observations on deterrence: not everything in the affairs of nations which might conceivably be called by the name; certainly not everything that has to do with deterring wrongdoers; but this one distinctive posture of threat with its unique features and paradoxical logic, to which the name "deterrence" and the corresponding concrete noun "deterrent" have in our time become especially appropriated.

When we call deterrence a "stance" or a "posture", the metaphorical character of these words helps us to look in two directions. On the one hand it directs our attention to the dispositions of military hardware: missile-bearing submarines cruising in certain waters, land-based missiles targeted on certain localities, missile-bearing aircraft with flight-paths prepared in certain directions. On the other hand it points to a set of attitudes, to ways in which we think about ourselves

and our adversaries and calculate our possible conduct in certain contingencies. Predictably it is these,
rather than the dispositions of hardware, that interest
the moralist more—though that remark must not be
taken to suggest that, from a moral point of view, the
hardware is a matter of indifference. The hardware
was invented to express the attitudes, and the attitudes in turn are reinforced by the hardware. Nevertheless, we may reasonably defend the moralist's priority. Deterrence is a pattern of *thinking* which governs
our discourse about international politics. Its importance as a moral theme is given in the way we conceive
our great geopolitical project. Most of us have only the
sketchiest knowledge of the hardware; but the attitudes of deterrence are the attitudes of the body
politic. They shape the categories within which our
political discourse is framed, the terms upon which
discussion can be joined; so that those who argue the
"unilateralist" case (so-called in the over-simplified
popular perception of the debate) are no less dependent than their opponents upon the common platitudes of deterrence. It is the platitudes which the
moralist must examine first, for they express the primary spiritual commitments which determine international life in our time.

"Deterrence": The Definitions

As soon as we embark on this discussion we face a terminological decision of some weight. We may use the
word "deterrence" more narrowly, to identify that

which is distinctive about our modern posture; or we may use it more widely to identify the continuity between what we do now and what states have always done. Like all such decisions, it is, on the one hand, *merely* terminological. That is to say, whichever convention we adopt, it will still be open to us to say the same things as if we had adopted the other one. Simple translation can be achieved by substituting the phrase "modern deterrence" for "deterrence" in the narrower sense, or by devising circumlocutions for "deterrence" in the broader sense, such as "ways of deterring aggression". However, like some other seemingly innocent quibbles, this one turns out to be critical in defining the scope of the discussion. When, for example, we read:

> Military deterrence is not something invented by the West for exclusively Western use; it is intrinsic to international conflict and the prospect of force throughout history; it is simply the means by which one State dissuades another from taking a hostile action by convincing it that the risks and costs imposed by counteraction will exceed any expected gains,[1]

we are immediately conscious that there are ends in view, good or bad, behind this apparently unremarkable stipulation of terms. On the most favourable reading it intends at least to keep before our eyes the practical demands of statecraft under any conditions of international order; it intends to force us to pay for our denunciations of modern deterrence by hard de-

1. Robert Osgood and Henning Wegener, *Deterrence: The Western Approach* (NATO Information Service, 1986), p. 2.

liberation about how states may deter their enemies justly and practicably. On a less favourable reading it intends to suggest that there is nothing, except perhaps an increment of scale, to distinguish our contemporary stance from those of past generations, thus fostering the illusion that what we do today is what has always been done.[2]

2. The cross-purposes to which the terminological difference may lead, as well as the legitimate concerns which may prompt a decision either way, are well-illustrated in an exchange between Paul Ramsey and Walter Stein from the now historic five-person debate published as *Peace, the Churches and the Bomb*, ed. James Finn (Council on Religion and International Affairs, 1965). Stein wrote: "Nothing short of a public government resolve to treat non-combatant populations as inviolable, whatever the circumstances—the dismantling, that is, of the whole ultimate foundation of deterrence—would now dismantle these built-in commitments to genocide on the part of its servants" (p. 22). Ramsey, in expressing general agreement with this statement, took exception to the phrase in parenthesis, and commented:

> There is good reason to believe that these steps would in no sense dismantle "the whole ultimate foundation of deterrence" ... He should have (investigated) ways in which weapons arsenals and systems might be corrected and reshaped into instruments of proper policy ... It ill behoves "moralists" to go about imbedding in the minds of people foolish and immoral notions about the necessary nature of deterrence or of modern war (p. 48).

I take it that the terminological discrepancy is clear: Stein uses "deterrence" in a narrow sense, Ramsey in a broader one; but this observation by no means resolves the disagreement, for each has a purpose in using the word as he does. Ramsey wishes to insist that if moral thinking is not to abdicate its re-

For my own part I propose to use the term "deterrence" in its narrower sense, highlighting what is distinctive about the form of the project that the modern age has conceived. But that is the purpose of these reflections as a whole: to point to the great intellectual gulf which divides what we do today from what states have traditionally done—and, we may add, still do when they are acting outside the constraints of East-West geopolitical opposition. The doubtful reader is not asked to accept anything on the basis of a terminological *coup* alone. Rather, the argument of these pages

---

sponsibilities, it must step forward and say how the modern state should deter its enemies justly. The point must be conceded. It is reasonable enough to be anxious if high denunciatory words manage to suggest, with a kind of fatalism, that there is nothing whatever to be done about modern weapons. But Stein can be read more sympathetically than that. A page later he wrote of the irrelevance of talk about "legitimate targets" ". . . without diagnosing the total, dynamic commitments we call the deterrent" (p. 24). That is to say, what has to be dismantled, and therefore first "diagnosed", is the nexus of *commitments*. Ramsey doubted that these commitments were embodied necessarily in the "weapons arsenals and systems" themselves; to which Stein might have replied that they were part of the deterrence-*idea* that has been culturally normative in the modern West. Can even the best-advised military and political leaders contend against a massive cultural assumption that determines, with a measure of necessity, the broad lines of public policy in our age? To bring this question forward is only to postpone, not to refuse, the task of deliberation about legitimate targets, etc., which will then follow in its proper place after the "diagnosis" of the cultural preconceptions which work to undermine such discussion and make it less than entirely serious.

is intended to demonstrate how this terminological decision makes good sense.

We are, at any rate, not free to define deterrence in whatever way we find convenient and then imagine that we have successfully discussed the idea which has come to dominate the political reasoning of our age. The point of a definition is to clear the way for a description; and a description must prove itself by its ability to shed light on the paradoxes and dilemmas of practical deliberation. To say that deterrence is what has always been done is to say that there are no new paradoxes and dilemmas of deterrence in our time—none, at any rate, which are more than simple variants on the age-old dilemma of Creon and Antigone. It is a difficult position to maintain in face of the self-consciously paradoxical character of much contemporary strategic thinking, generated in part, if I am not mistaken, by sheer intellectual inebriation at the capacity of certain analytical techniques to produce counter-intuitive results. If, however, deterrence as we moderns think of it is a new idea and not a perennial one, then it is necessary to grapple with its historical development and the intellectual milieu that has produced it. We are defining not a term but a historical movement of thought.

In order to encompass that consideration, we need to frame a definition that has two forms: one to describe the mature shape of the idea as it has developed, the other to identify the core notion which has given the development its unity. That core notion, I propose, is this: that the traditional use of menaces to preserve the peace *can be rendered entirely effective when the menaces are infinitely enhanced.* Around this notion has grown a broader tradition of strategic thinking which is marked by the assumption that *threats may exceed the limits of what it would make sense to do.* This looser description encompasses most of what the deterrence-idea has become (though not quite all, since it has suffered internal degeneration into a war-fighting proposal, as we shall see in chapter 3); the former, tighter one identifies the premise which sustains its logic. The logic of deterrence is paradoxical because it rests on the idea that order can be ensured by a posture of wilful irrationality.[3] The central question posed by the theory of deterrence, then, can be captured in the quotation from Jane Austen which I set on the frontispiece: "My Emma! . . . what is the certainty of caprice?"

A conception which emerges directly from this account of the deterrence-idea is that what is undertaken, planned and purposed in the issuing of deterrent threats is notionally and morally different from what would be undertaken, planned and purposed in putting those threats into action. There is a disjunction between the act of threatening and the act of execution. This is implied in the thought that the threat itself, if sufficiently inflated, is a means of ensuring against the need to carry it out. What has happened, in fact, in the articulation of modern deterrence, is that the deterring of aggressors has ceased to be seen as a

3. Cf. David Hollenbach, *Nuclear Ethics* (Paulist Press, 1983), p. 65: "Deterrence policy . . . uses irrationality as a tool of political reason."

subsidiary moment in the larger complex of political action based on force, and has come to be thought of as a self-sustaining activity in isolation from political action based on force. Why and how this change of perspective occurred we will have occasion to explore further in chapter 2. But the extent of the change is clear enough whenever we hear it said that modern weapons, by virtue of their immense destructiveness, are not to be thought of as war-fighting weapons in the usual sense.[4] An opposition has been set up between two possible uses of weapons: deterring is now something *else* that we may use them for.

In current discussion this disjunction is often expressed by saying that there are two quite different ways of *intending* acts of war: the *hypothetical* intention that is involved in the purpose of deterring aggression and the *actual* intention which would be involved in warmaking itself. "There is no logical relationship", one apologist writes,

> between the intention to use the deterrent formed in circumstances where only having that intention will in fact ensure that it need never be used, and the intention to use the deterrent in circumstances where it has already failed . . . The advocate of the deterrent will certainly say that he fully intends to use nuclear weapons should he be attacked. In so saying he is not

---

4. Cf. Osgood and Wegener, *Deterrence*, p. 2: "Indeed, their capacity to inflict costs that an adversary will regard as far out of proportion to any gains it might derive from a hostile action put them outside the familiar category of war-fighting weapons intended only to defeat an enemy militarily."

... logically committed to giving the same answer in the quite different circumstances which would obtain if he were attacked.[5]

At a later point we will return to the specific form of the question that is raised here. For our present purposes it is enough to point out that this distinction springs directly from the primitive disjunction between deterrence and war, which is at the heart of the modern idea. An argument like this is more than a clever debating manoeuvre; it expresses the very soul of deterrence. And that poses a difficulty for would-be critics which is often underestimated.

The Classic Criticism

What we may call the "classic" mode of criticising deterrence approaches the subject by way of the moral principles which govern acts of war. It evaluates the acts of war which are the content of the deterrent threat and finds them wanting. But then it risks being deflected: the negative verdict it pronounces on these threatened acts of war is irrelevant, for it is a verdict on something different, something still hypothetical,

5. Gerard Hughes, "The Intention to Deter", in *The Cross and the Bomb*, ed. Francis Bridger (Mowbray, 1983), pp. 33f. Cf. Richard Harries, "The Morality of Nuclear Deterrence", in *What Hope in an Armed World?*, ed. Richard Harries (Pickering & Inglis, 1982), p. 100: "If it is true that deterrence and its failure are fundamentally different situations, it is misleading to apply the morality of the use of weapons in a wooden way to the morality of possession and threatened use."

and not a verdict on deterrence itself, which precisely does *not* purpose such acts of war but only to maintain the peace. This deflection of the criticism is so important to an understanding of modern deterrence that I shall delay a little longer over the difficulties the classical critic must face and use them as an excuse to introduce my own, rather different approach.

The moral principles said to govern acts of war are generally derived by contemporary writers from some version of the "just war theory" of sixteenth- and seventeenth-century provenance, which has enjoyed a marked revival in a past half-century among English-speaking moralists of Christian inspiration. (The other major contemporary tradition for evaluating acts of war is utilitarian, and with this we need not be concerned since its adherents are unlikely to favour this indirect route into a critique of deterrence.) The two criteria to be met by any act of war, according to this account, are, first, that it should not intend to take innocent lives (in effect, the lives of non-belligerents)—though it may happen that they perish, and foreseeably so, in the course of an attack which intends only the destruction of a military objective; and second, that the evil it inflicts should be less grave than the evil it seeks to avert. These are the commonly-called principles of "discrimination" and "proportion". Of the two the former has an operative priority in deliberation, in that its application to any particular decision we have to make is immediate, not open to disputable calculation. Either we are, or we are not, proposing to kill innocents, and there are no two ways about it; whereas the question whether an act of war is worth its cost is always a matter of difficult and carefully-weighed judgment.

It might appear a straightforward matter to bring the charge that modern deterrence, which rests upon the deployment of missiles powerful enough to swallow up whole metropolitan areas with their inhabitants, constitutes a sustained threat to ignore the principle of discrimination, i.e. to commit murder. But the logic of this charge needs some care. The problem with it emerges clearly if we make the comparison between a nuclear attack on a city, which *may* be indiscriminate, and a method of warfare which is *categorically* indiscriminate: the use of biochemical weapons to destroy a population through its water- or food-supplies. In the case of the nuclear attack it would still be relevant to ask whether the deaths of the inhabitants of the city were intended, or whether they were merely foreseen as "collateral" to an interest in the destruction of a military target; but it would make no sense to ask such a question about the poisoning of food and water, which strikes immediately at the ordinary life-sustaining functions of a community's existence. The answering of the question, of course, does not depend at all on the psychological rationalisations of those who order or execute the destruction, but on the practical rationality of the act itself. There can be a perfectly intelligible military rationale for the destruction of a city which has nothing to do with wanting its citizens dead (as end or as means): the elimination, for example, of a hardened underground missile-site located somewhere uncertain within the city's boundaries. There can be no rationale for poisoning food and water which does not imply wanting the population dead, even if only as a means to the end of military victory.

The critic's difficulty is that in assessing a decision that others have taken, or might take, to attack a city, he cannot apply the principle of discrimination with the same immediacy as if it were his own decision, on the one hand, or as if it were a categorically indiscriminate decision, on the other. He does not know merely by looking that the death of non-combatants was intended in the attack. He can only show by elimination that its conduct was such as to admit of no reasonable alternative explanation. He depends upon the failure of any account which would credit the actors with intent to discriminate: *either* an account which holds the deaths of the non-combatants to have been proportionate and justifiable, *or* an account which accepts that they were disproportionate, but attributes this outcome to error of judgment or negligence rather than to murderous malice. But this elimination of alternative accounts is precisely what cannot be done in the case of hypothetical future acts of war, the details of which are as yet undetermined. We can say of a city-destroying capacity that it *might* be used indiscriminately; perhaps also, as the Vatican Council said, that it might provide an "occasion" for our using it indiscriminately; and perhaps even that the likelihood of an opportunity for discriminate use is so remote that we can hardly justify our keeping it. But whatever weight that last observation may have as a counsel of prudence, it falls short of the categorical criticism that was envisaged.

There is, however, a further step that the classic

critic may take. Granted that discriminate use of this capacity is conceivable in the abstract, is it not belied, he may ask, in the project of deterrence itself, simply because it proceeds by *menacing* the adversary with the massive numbers of non-combatant dead which must result—dead which were supposed to be "collateral" casualties of the military purpose?

> Assume that all deaths of non-combatants would be incidental to the destruction of legitimate military targets. Even so, it is clear that many (at least) of the deaths *intended in* the threats of city-swapping and final retaliation are *not intended as* the killing of combatants, and are thus *intended* as the killing of innocents . . . Massive destruction of people including non-combatants is part of what Western leaders desire the Soviet leadership to fear . . . Since what they desire the other side to fear is what they threaten, and . . . what they threaten is what they intend, they intend the killing of innocents.[6]

6. John Finnis, Joseph M. Boyle, and Germain Grisez, *Nuclear Deterrence, Morality and Realism* (Clarendon Press, 1987), p. 92. The case for an immediate judgment of indiscriminacy is unlikely to find abler advocates than these authors, so we may take it that the signs of strain in their argument are systemic. The discussion from which the quotation is taken begins (p. 91) from the reiterated Western intention of attacking cities, and then dismisses as irrelevant the suggestion that the deaths of non-combatants in such attacks might be unintended. They defend this step on the grounds that "targeting does not define intent". They proceed with two arguments for this principle: first, the one that I have quoted; second, the argument that at Hiroshima the means used was manifestly in excess of what was required to destroy the modest military in-

Each of the two linked clauses introduced by the word "since" in the final sentence of that quotation needs careful scrutiny. We will return to the second presently; here we are concerned with the first— "what they desire the other side to fear is what they threaten"—and will test it with an analogy. Suppose

---

stallations. The principle itself is unexceptionable. It is not merely where the weapon was aimed, but the whole internal ordering of the act including the scale of the means chosen, the reasonable judgments that could plausibly have been made about the urgency of the military threat, etc., that leaves us in no doubt that the purpose of the attack on Hiroshima was to kill non-combatants on a grand scale as a means to securing military victory. We conclude it from the actual disproportion of the military means to the supposed military rationale. But when the authors tell us that in any future nuclear attack on a city "the same would be true" (p. 94), they are telling us something which we may reasonably fear, but cannot reasonably claim to know, about the future. Their own alternative to the doctrine that targeting defines intent is too loose: "An action or aspect of an action is intentional if it is part of the plan on which one freely acts. That is to say, what one tries to bring about in acting, whether it be the goal one seeks to realise or the means one chooses to realise that goal, is intended" (p. 79). They would have done better to write: "part of the plan *of the action* which one performs" and "what one tries to bring about *by one's action*", since it is the scope of the act itself which determines its intention, and not any hope that one may, or may not, form about what may follow from it. It is surprising to find these well-known opponents of consequentialism dismissing the relevance of the distinction between intended and foreseen-but-unintended consequences! From this they proceed to condemn—not too loudly, but too uncircumspectly—the Western deterrent for its intention that Soviets

that a magistrate is giving a severe warning to an offender who is now for the second time receiving a lightish sentence on a not minor charge. "The next time you appear before me", he says, "I will have no alternative but to send you to prison. I want you to consider very carefully not only what this will mean for you, but the *quite undeserved misery* that it will bring upon your wife and children." In this instance what the magistrate desires the offender to fear is something rather more than what he threatens. He threatens imprisonment, which would be justified; but he desires him to fear also the unjustified suffering of his family which must follow as a necessary consequence. Yet he could hardly be said to *threaten* this injustice to the family, and certainly not in any sense that would authorise us to conclude that he *intended* it. So it is with the threats of deterrence. The fact that a state wants

---

should fear "not denial of their military objectives by enemy defensive measures but . . . *unacceptable losses* 'at whatever level of nuclear conflict'" (p. 94). The emphasis is theirs, and is misplaced. The final phrase should have been emphasised, for it expresses the purpose of enhancing the threat *to any degree necessary to make the losses unacceptable*. From that purposed disproportioning of the means to the proper political ends one may infer murderous intent. The desire to impose "unacceptable losses" in itself, even if they include collateral noncombatant deaths, does not express more than the reasonable hope that a proportioned attack against a legitimate target will prove to be an unacceptable prospect to the enemy. And when did the classical exponents of just-war theory ever make the mistake of saying that the only proper intention of an act of war is "denial of (the enemy's) military objectives by . . . defensive measures"?

its enemy to fear the massive civilian losses which must follow even a proportionate attack on a military target does not mean that it intends those losses. We must be careful to differentiate this distinction from the one between hypothetical and actual intention which lies at the heart of deterrence-theory. Within the terms of our analogy the hypothetical intention is to send the offender to prison ("the next time you appear before me"); and that evil, if it were to be inflicted, would be inflicted intentionally. But of the injustice to the family we have to say that it is not "inflicted" at all, but simply arises from the circumstances; and the only thing the magistrate intends in respect of it is that it should be seen to be inevitable, and feared appropriately.

The charge of threatening murder, then, cannot be brought against the posture of deterrence immediately; but that does not mean that it cannot be brought at all. For as in the case of past acts of war we may sometimes infer murderous intent by eliminating other explanations, so it is in the case of threatened future acts of war, even indeterminate ones. The threat of an act of destruction which would lack any possible rationale as a proportioned attack on a legitimate target, on the one hand, and in which the disproportion could not reasonably be ascribed to misjudgment or error, on the other, would properly be thought of as a threat of murder. In excusing "misjudgment", of course, we do not forget that there are some misjudgments which are not excusable, and which themselves could constitute a ground for the charge of murderous intent. We expect military and political decision-makers to bring at least a moderate moral sensibility to their decisions, and if they fail to give evidence of this we suppose that they have been corrupted by the doctrine of military necessity. A decision to use a nuclear weapon which killed large numbers of civilians might be judged murderous, *even if* it were defended in good faith as collateral and proportionate, if that defence were thought to be too implausible for anyone of moderate moral sensibility to credit it. One may commit murder by holding another's life at risk for a trifle. Similarly one may be indiscriminate in military action if one reckons the lives of non-combatants of less importance than a moderately sensitive person could possibly reckon them. And in the case of prospective, threatened attacks the same judgment would be in place if no moderately sensitive person could conceive that the likely damage could be justified by any military or political gain.

I take it, for example, that if anybody learns, even in outline, what is generally expected to follow from the explosion of 6.33 megatons simultaneously in two hundred Soviet cities, and learns also of the longer-term results which might quite probably ensue from such explosions over subsequent decades but which cannot be predicted with certainty, then—even without bringing into consideration the prospect of a reprisal attack of the same magnitude—he is likely to know immediately that no conceivable goal of human endeavour could be served by it. From this he may conclude that none of the political goods for which we strive in international politics and war could be served by it; and from this in turn that no proportionate military purpose could be served by it (since military purposes are at the service of political ends) and that no reasonable person who understood what military activity was for could ever mistake such an attack for a proportioned military action. From this he may conclude, again, that (apart from the wilder type of soldier portrayed in doomsday movies, who has very probably forgotten what military activity was for) anybody who threatens such an attack threatens what he knows to be an act of destruction without military, political, or human reason; and, finally, that since the one who knows this even as he makes his threat must reckon that he will *still* know it should he ever come to make the threat good, he threatens to commit murder.

This instance will serve as a paradigm for a range of other threatened acts of lesser gravity. I will not venture to guess how far down the scale of destruction such immediate certainty prevails, though I presume that it must be some considerable way. There are, however, some categorically disproportionate actions which could not be classified as murder, even though they may, in their kind, be quite as wicked. The threat conveyed by an automatic-launch-on-warning system, for example, because it by-passes the threat of murderous *decision*, would be better thought of as a threat to go mad and relinquish control. Again, there may be threats of force which one would judge probably disproportionate in almost every circumstance, if not categorically disproportionate in all. Such a threat one might wish to judge as gravely imprudent, which is not necessarily a weak criticism if one has formed a proper assessment of the role of prudence in politics. It was a judicious observation of Paul Ramsey that war "becomes a disproportionate means to any substantive political purposes long before it need be judged to have become indiscriminate".[7] For the critic this means simply that he cannot expect to find one moral term, such as "murder", which will do to condemn any and every unjustified threat that is issued under the general rubric of deterrence. He is expected to use some discrimination on his own behalf. Nevertheless, there are aspects of our deterrence posture which are rightly said to threaten indiscriminate attack upon the innocent, and the case for this conclusion will be strengthened as we develop our thesis that in modern deterrence the disproportion of the threat is deliberately enhanced.

The Inner Fortress of Deterrence

The classic critic of deterrence may go this far. But this is not yet where he wants to be. He has laid the charge of murder against the act that is threatened but not against the act of threatening. He has yet to prove the second clause of the sentence in the quotation: "since . . . what they threaten is what they intend . . ." And

7. "A Political Ethics Context for Strategic Thinking", in *Strategic Thinking and its Moral Implications*, ed. M. A. Kaplan (University of Chicago Press, 1973), p. 144. Reprinted in Ramsey's *Speak Up for Just War or Pacifism* (Pennsylvania State University Press, 1988), p. 209.

here he comes up against the inner fortress of deter-rence-theory, its peculiar assumption that the deter-rent state can transcend the belligerent content of its threats in the pacific intent of its threatening. The state's will to deter, it is claimed, is at arms-length from the disproportion contained in the threat; it deploys it only hypothetically to yield a prospect of disaster that will ensure the keeping of the peace. Somehow the critic must penetrate this remote detachment of the will to deter, its claim to be free to deploy in hypothe-sis what it could not be free to deploy in act. And this cannot be done quickly by arguments that are con-ceived as brushing aside a quibble about intention. For even if these arguments are successful on their own terms, they do not get to the bottom of what makes the assumption of transcendence persuasive. We have first to understand deterrence-theory as a philosophy; it must be coaxed into giving us its reasons. We may return later to the question of whether it is mistaken about intention when we have first met it fully upon its own ground.

Deep within our cultural tradition there is a thrust towards practical transcendence which provides a setting in which the transcendence claimed for the de-terrent will becomes explicable. That is my reason for approaching deterrence as a form of the modern tradition of practical thinking which we have come to call"technology".[8] For in technology we find a context

8. In *Begotten or Made?* (Clarendon Press, 1984) I defined technology in terms of the idea of acting as making, the facet most applicable to questions of artificial reproduction with

for all the elements which make modern deterrence-theory distinctive. Deterrence is about how the behaviour of nations can be subjected to management, by taking the infinite into our threats and by deploying the calculated prospect of human action and reaction as an instrument to ensure predictability. In describing it we are not bound to speak of the *particular* techniques which currently serve it (the "technologies" in the vulgar sense), though, of course, those techniques characteristically embody and represent it.[9] The idea of deterrence was in our minds before it gave rise to nuclear weapons; it could continue to be there when nuclear weapons have been rendered obsolete by the advent of some more economical deterrent. And, we may add, not everything included in the term "nuclear weapons" is a deterrent-weapon in the narrow sense, incapable of rational military use.

---

which I was concerned. But it can be approached by way of other conceptions: that means, rather than ends, have become the controlling factor in practical deliberation (Ellul); that contemplation has been supplanted by will (Grant); or that we are in the grip of "Utopian dynamics" (Jonas). If forced to reduce the complex group of ideas which distinguish modern practical reasoning to a single phrase, I would venture "unlimited practical transcendence".

9. When the Vatican Fathers wrote (*Gaudium et Spes*, 80) that nuclear weapons afforded "a kind of occasion for perpetrating (the) abominations" of indiscriminate total warfare (*The Documents of Vatican II*, ed. W. M. Abbott [Geoffrey Chapman, 1967], p. 294), they were understating the matter. They might have said that the policy of threatening indiscriminate war was the occasion for nuclear weapons.

The idea of deterrence is given in the technological conception of human action and its relation to the world.

This approach to the topic will probably appear arbitrary to those who either have not grasped, or are not willing to concede, the qualitative differences that technology has introduced into our practical reasoning. Of course, it is true that warnings of unlimited evil have been part of the rhetoric of persuasion from time immemorial. What is distinctive in modern deterrence is that the limitless evil which imagination can propose in relation to any determined threat has become a project for practical execution; and this is necessarily a modern development since the appearance of the limitless within the scope of practical deliberation is a modern development in Western culture. In pre-technological ages the rhetoric of limitlessness gave an imaginative depth to projects of finite, even if terrible, reprisals. Our forefathers at their best consciously aimed to limit the sanctions of war; at their worst they set out to inflict them with the utmost inhumanity. But neither at their best nor at their worst did they undertake to transcend the inherent limits of human action. What they did and what they suffered belonged within a scheme of things, bounded by the great impersonal permanence of nature, and yielded a story that could be told and wept over by later generations of mankind who shared with them the common terms of human existence. "Through all the years immutable stands this event"—so ends the Greek tragedy. "He established them for ever and ever; he fixed their bounds which cannot be passed"—so runs the Hebrew psalm.[10] In nature and history they discerned permanencies which set terms for human action which they could not conceive of challenging. We can and do conceive of it.

What we cannot do, of course, even in the modern era, is to conceive of such practical transcendence *responsibly*. We cannot comprehend within our striving to overcome our limits the true relations of ourselves with each other, with nature, and with God. So there is this, but only this, to be said for the generally preposterous rhetoric which has gained some currency in theological circles about our new power to undo the work of God in creation: on the one hand, our technical resources admit the project of making the earth unfit for human habitation; on the other, these resources are the fruit of a century or more of cultural preoccupation with rendering human action infinite. The titanic thought has been facilitated in the modern age by the philosophical conditions of late idealism and by the technical powers (responding to the philosophical conditions, not anticipating them) which have permitted us to build a kind of shadow-infinity into our actions in the form of world encompassing damage. But there is illusion at the heart of this technological titanism. "He that dwelleth in heaven shall laugh them to scorn."[11] We may, I suppose, debate the question whether the capacity for species–self-destruction that we now dispose of is a true mirror-

10. Sophocles, *Oedipus at Colonus,* in *The Theban Plays,* tr. E. F. Watling (Penguin Books, 1947), lines 1778-79; Psalm 148:6.
11. Psalm 2:4.

image of the capacity for species–self-deification that we once dreamed of. But theologians who are too lacking in a sense of irony to appreciate the fierce humour in this outcome of our strivings are hardly in a position to say much about creation. Creation may be sure of its own vindication. It receives it in the judgment of that terrible laughter that is never closer to us than when we talk of our power to destroy the world.

These remarks indicate sufficiently the interest which the moral theologian, as a theologian, has in deterrence. As a moralist, of course, he is interested in any deliberative question which his contemporaries find difficult. But in this case Christian theology has a distinct perspective from which to interpret the difficulties illuminatingly, a perspective which arises from its ongoing controversy with the human race about the being and authority of God. The issue of deterrence leads us straight back to that question; and if the theologian judges it to be especially urgent, that is not owing to the threat of ecocatastrophe but to the perennial urgency of the question of God itself. An inadequate theological response to deterrence is a betrayal at the heart of the theologian's mission.[12]

12. Theologians had better spare themselves the trouble of observing the distinctiveness of modern practical reasoning, if, when they have done so, they can do no better than treat its more idolatrous pretensions with literal-minded seriousness. Of the thesis that our power to uncreate creation has the positive theological virture of requiring us to deconstruct the notion of God as creator (cf. Gordon Kaufmann, *Theology for a Nuclear Age* [Westminster Press, 1985]), we can say only that the theologian who proposes this either intends his pro-

Nor will it assist that mission if Christian thinkers allow themselves to be persuaded too easily that as a matter of course deterrence can be made subject to the disciplines appropriate to the restraint of evil.[13] We

---

posal seriously—in which case we expect to see him treat the task of educating us to be gods and to wield the powers of providence with the greatest urgency—or he is merely trifling with serious matters.

13. This assumption seems to lie behind Richard Harries's insistence that "whatever targeting policy may have been in the past . . . the point is that now and in the future it must be both discriminate and proportionate" (*Christianity and War in a Nuclear Age* [Mowbray, 1986], p. 134). Grateful as we must be for this demand, we can only shake our heads over its intelligibility. Disproportion is not an accident of modern deterrence; it is the principle on which it is thought. I address this criticism to this author especially, since of all those who have undertaken to defend NATO policies to the church in recent years, none has been so determined to establish good faith with the Christian tradition of discourse about the moral limits of war. He has failed, I would judge, to appreciate the debt of the deterrence-idea to the idealist tradition for which, as a Niebuhrian realist, he expresses disdain, and so has failed to comprehend the full scope of the idea as it has actually come to prevail among us. It is, of course, all too easy to be carried along by assurances which those who speak for NATO, officially or unofficially, are ready to offer at this point. Consider, for example, the words of Osgood and Wegener, whom I take to speak for NATO policy though their document has no official standing: "Any conceivable use of nuclear weapons would . . . be governed by the law of proportionality between attack and defensive action, and by the prohibition of deliberate attack against civilian populations only" (*Deterrence*, p. 11). What has been meant morally by the demand of proportion is not adequately safeguarded in this statement. It concerns the pro-

should certainly find no fault with the proposal that the traditional disciplines of just-war theory are sources of relevant moral wisdom for the understanding of deterrence. Nor should we object to the reminder, characteristic of Christian "realists" who have learned from Reinhold Niebuhr, that Christian thought must always confess the obligation to restrain evil since it acknowledges the hard truth of the doctrine of original sin. The question, rather, is whether we invoke at this point a concept of original sin extensive enough to encompass the insights of Isaiah 14 and Ezekiel 28. Original sin must not be reduced to a presumption of social imperfectability, though such a presumption is implied by it. It has to do also with the constant yearning of human politics for the seat of divinity and the exercise of omnipotence. This yearning arises both in the evil we resist and in the evil with which we resist evil. There is no safe place from

---

portionate ordering of an act to its proper military and political ends, not merely an equation of force, tit for tat, all the way up the scale of violence. The demand of discrimination *might* be represented adequately here if, but only if, one abstracted these words from the general context of accepted disproportion. Even so, however, one would have to discover how this assurance was meant to be understood in the light of the aim attributed to the "general nuclear response" on p. 5: "degrading the aggressor's capability and will to continue aggression". Such words are usually taken to imply a direct attack on civilian morale by acts of counter-population warfare. For the disingenuousness of some of these reassurances see Finnis, Boyle and Grisez, *Nuclear Deterrence, Morality and Realism*, pp. 18-27, though these authors carry their hermeneutic of suspicion a shade too far.

which we can go out to do battle with original sin in
confidence that it has placed no double-agents in our
company. The best Christian political thought, Niebuhr's included, emphasises the need to set up restraints in both directions, against evil and against the
evil implicit in the restraint of evil. Original sin
demands both the practice of a tough-minded "realist" politics founded on the possibility of force, and of
a "just" politics founded on the disciplines that constrain force to the service of the common good.

The seductive appeal of deterrence-theory to
thinkers of the realist tradition lies in its conception of
the enemy as one who cannot be made susceptible to
the codes of honour and rational political interest
which generally govern relations among states. Here,
surely, is the supreme challenge to our tough-minded-
ness! Only those who can bring themselves to admit
that such an enemy may exist and may need to be resisted have any right to class themselves as "realists"
from now on! They alone are the true believers in de-
pravity! A great deal has been written, of course, about
whether the Soviet Union represents this kind of
enemy, some of it is careful and well judged but much
of it is steeped in prejudice. The answer to that question, however, is irrelevant. For if the Soviet Union is
not that kind of enemy, then some other state on some
other occasion may be. In speculation, at least, the
worst-case scenario is the right one to follow, since it
defines the outer limits of practical rationality. (In concrete political judgments, on the other hand, it is usually more prudent *not* to presume the worst.) The important question is not whether the worst case has

actually been realised by Soviet intentions, but whether, if it were, the predictions and recommendations of deterrence would give adequate guidance on how to deal with it. The mischief done by preoccupation with the motives of the Soviets is that the sudden rush of realism to the head in this regard disinclines the true-believing realist from being equally realistic about deterrence. Yet deterrence itself invites some critical examination in the light of the doctrine of original sin.

One of the tasks of the political theologian in any age is to discern the Antichrist—that is to say, to trace within the movements of his own time the heaving shape of the titanic aspiration which challenges the throne of God. Niebuhr believed that he had traced it within the strident idealist pacifism, with its belief in human perfectibility, of the inter-war years; his characterisation certainly had a measure of persuasiveness. The question I have to raise in this essay concerns the debt of deterrence to precisely the same idealist tradition.

In a seminal remark penned in 1964, Paul Ramsey observed: "There is nothing more like a pacifist than a believer in massive deterrence. Both think it possible to banish the use of force from human history."[14] My argument will be that deterrence is, in fact, a tough-minded mutation of pacifism, a pacifism transformed by a technological and historicist vision of human progress. Many of the traditional arguments made against pacifism are also *mutatis mutandis* arguments

14. *The Just War* (Scribners, 1968), p. 141.

against deterrence. The clearest demonstration of the spiritual affinity between the two philosophies lies in the historical roots of the deterrence-idea, to which I turn now. It was formed out of the war-sickness of the late eighteenth and early nineteenth centuries, and was finally offered to the Western world in the twentieth as the realisation of a goal long sought: the banishment of force from human history.

CHAPTER II

Growth

THE END of the eighteenth century was a period of war-weariness and cynicism about war. Among the practical philosophers it was a period of speculation about how a "perpetual peace" might be established. It was also the period in which a nascent philosophy of history began to open the eyes of thinkers to discern an immanent purposiveness in the development of Western culture. Even war, we find it thought, must have its purpose. But that purpose is not the functional purpose traditionally ascribed to it, of providing a sanction for peaceable and ordered relations among nations, but a purpose *in history*, which is to cancel itself out. "Nature", Kant wrote,

> has once more used human quarrelsomeness . . . as a means of discovering a state of calm and security. That is, through wars, through excessive and never remitting preparation for war, through the resultant distress that every nation must, even during times of peace, feel within itself, they are driven to make some initial attempts; finally, after much devastation, upheaval, and even complete exhaustion of their

inner powers, they are driven to take the step that reason could have suggested . . . namely, to leave the law-
less state of savagery and enter into a federation of
peoples.[1]

This was the intellectual soil in which the deterrence-
idea, as I shall try to describe it, first germinated: war
was the cruel sport of factious princes; yet historical
dialectic could illuminate an element of usefulness
even in war.[2]

The deterrence-idea itself, however, involves one
further thought: that there is especial usefulness (in
forwarding the historical dialectic) in the indefinite
enlargement of the scale upon which preparations for

1. Immanuel Kant, "Idea for a Universal History with a
Cosmopolitan Intent" (Prussian Academy ed. 8.24). Tr. Ted
Humphrey in *Perpetual Peace and Other Essays* (Hackett, 1983),
p. 34. The classical doctrine, common to Augustine and
Grotius, that the proper end of war was peace, could appear
superficially as an antecedent to Kant's theory—but only if
one overlooked the transformation of the meaning of the
word "end" which was effected by the new theory of history.
2. I doubt the suggestion of Ian Clark (*Limited Nuclear War*
[Martin Robertson, 1982], pp. 15f.) that already in the seven-
teenth century Samuel Pufendorf had considered the argument that a brutally fought war will be shorter, and therefore
conform better to natural law, than a generously fought one.
Pufendorf's discussion is concerned only with the subject of
limited *truces* concluded during the conduct of a war, which
"do but increase and nourish war"; he does not argue for or
against the more general contention that unrestrained war is
shorter. Nevertheless, I make no claim to identify the very ear-
liest buds on the stock of the deterrence-idea, merely to indicate the general period and milieu in which they began to appear.

war are mounted. The deterrence-idea is a technological idea, dependent on the modern concept of an infinitely expanded scope of human action. It goes beyond the pre-modern practical theories of war, in which the task of deterring aggression was fully accounted for within the terms of "defence" and "punishment", notions which do not suppose any theory of history to support them; but it also goes beyond the historicist optimism which is purely speculative in orientation, in that it offers a technique for forwarding the goal of history, and so turns history into a practical project. That technique is to take the infinite into our sanctions, which, by becoming categorically disproportionate to all conceivable human goals and enterprises, will ensure the reduction, or even the abolition of war.

Schleiermacher: The Eclipse of Virtue

The first hesitant articulation of the deterrence-idea of which I am personally aware comes from the first half of the nineteenth century, in a couple of pages in Schleiermacher's *Christliche Sitte*, published posthumously in 1843.[3] Schleiermacher has expressed the view that the death-penalty should be unthinkable for

3. Schleiermacher's involvement in the same patriotic Berlin circles as Clausewitz may suggest a provenance for the idea. See P. Paret, *Clausewitz and the State* (Clarendon Press, 1976), pp. 167, 212. I am indebted to Dr. Anne Loades for this reference. The argument in *Christliche Sitte* appears on pp. 280-82 of the Leipzig edition of Schleiermacher's *Werke*.

a Christian state, and now he faces a difficulty: that war, too, like the death-penalty, appears to be directed explicitly to the taking of the enemy's life. But this, he argues, is not the case. War is directed by one state against another with the end of avenging a wrong done or of establishing a secure situation for the future. It proceeds by attempting so to weaken the enemy that he has no reasonable course of action left to him but to comply with the demands that are made upon him. There is no interest in killing his citizens as such; it must be regarded as accident rather than design if he suffers extensive loss of life. It is not the intention or policy of the belligerent state, but the consequence of the enemy's own arbitrary determination to resist. So far we have an entirely recognisable deployment of the traditional principle of double-effect; but here Schleiermacher makes a new departure into historicism. War, he concedes, used not to be as he describes it now, in the days when men fought with sword and lance. But modern war, he argues, which depends upon artillery, is unquestionably nobler, in that it avoids instant recourse to life-and-death struggle and merely indicates to the enemy the appropriateness of withdrawing before the concentration of natural force which has been brought to bear.

In the 1830's gunpowder was some half a millennium old; but when Schleiermacher looked at it he saw something new in it, something more than merely extending the damage beyond that which could be done with sword and lance. He saw *disproportion*. Between two warriors armed with sword and lance there is a proportion, so that the challenge to fight evokes human virtues of courage and bravery. Replace those weapons with artillery, and the proportion is destroyed, even if they are armed equally. There is no proportion between the force which is brought to bear and the human courage which it might evoke. Firepower cannot be resisted by human virtue, but can only crush it. Schleiermacher was among the first to make the announcement that in modern war there is no place for honour; and he made it without the slightest regret. To remove honour and virtue from the equation of force is pure gain, for it takes away all *reason* to resist superior force, and thus ensures that fighting will not happen, lives will not be lost. Resistance now becomes "arbitrary". Schleiermacher's seed thought, which will grow into the doctrine of deterrence, is that the disproportion between the enhanced scope of the techniques of force and the limits of human virtue is useful; it is an instrument to avert war and ensure peace. His thought was "technological", even though the technique in question was ancient, for he discerned new possibilities in it for refashioning the relations between states and putting them on a new footing.

It is a matter of no importance whether artillery warfare, as Schleiermacher knew it, actually *could* so overwhelm human virtue as to render it irrelevant to war. Once the idea had been born, the technical development could pursue it. But even this idea, new as it was, did not arise without antecedent or presupposition. Lying behind it are two related conceptions, which, by Schleiermacher's time, had already been present in the Western consciousness for two centuries. One is that in extreme circumstances virtue is irrelevant to rational human action, since practical reason works solely to one end, that of self-preservation. The other is that this reduction of all rationality to the fear of death is the basis on which political order of every kind is established. These are, of course, the ground-rules of contractarian political thought as articulated most famously by Hobbes. The transition from the state of nature to that of civil society is effected on the basis of each individual's fear of death. Within civil society there is scope enough for virtue and for a widely conceived morality and rationality; but these are derivative from the prior fact of civil order. Faced with the disappearance of that order, rational behaviour is reduced to this one point, that one should take all measures necessary to protect one's life. This provides a basis for the recovery of civil order. Schleiermacher's is a simple application of the Hobbesian principles, which he has himself articulated a few pages earlier. "Even war," he tells us, "is no more than the preparation for a state of international law, no more than the means to evoke it and make the need for it more keenly felt."[4] These principles are reinforced with the technological insight that force disproportionate to human virtue can ensure that the fear of

4. *Werke,* Leipzig ed., p. 277. My account draws out only one aspect of Schleiermacher's thinking about war, the one in which he is heir to the contractarian tradition. Another aspect, more Grotian, envisages war arising within the context of international law and as a means to uphold it. My aim is not to do justice to him as a thinker but to trace the intellectual history of the one thought.

death, and with it the recovery of civil order, must prevail.

Schleiermacher's remarks take the form of a defense of "modern" war, by which he meant the classical artillery-war. Among his contemporaries there was a sharper awareness of how artillery-war had evolved, precisely in the first half of the nineteenth century, into a phenomenon that was "modern" in a more precise sense. The French Revolution, with its use of the *levée en masse*, the campaigns of Napoleon and the guerilla operations of the Peninsular War, all gave complexion to Clausewitz's assertion that "real warfare" had made "its appearance in . . . absolute completeness just in our own times".[5] By "absoluteness" Clausewitz meant what we would call its character as "total war", involving whole populations rather than professional armies only. It was war "waged with the whole weight of the national power on each side" and with "violence pushed to its utmost bounds".[6]

Tolstoy: Excess as a Means of Restraint

In this development lay a further element of disproportion, which both necessitated and invited a reformulation of Schleiermacher's insight. The success of modern war in limiting itself, he had thought,

5. C. von Clausewitz, *On War*, tr. J. J. Graham (Routledge & Kegan Paul, 1956), 3:81.
6. Ibid., 1:231; 1:4.

sprang from the disproportion between force and virtue. The weakness of this account was that it assumed too individualistic a view of human motivation, and did not allow for the power of mass political aspirations, which could cheerfully sacrifice both individual virtue and individual life to the achievement of the common good. Yet the enhanced ferocity of total warfare offered a new purchase on the useful disproportion, which would operate for peaceful restraint when the ferocity of war outweighed the political goals of populations. Thus Francis Lieber, the American strategic theorist whose thought shaped the way in which the civil war was fought, wrote in 1838 that the traditional restraints on the conduct of war provoked the inception of wars for "trifling or unjust causes". It was "not only right but (the) duty" of a belligerent power "to resort to the most destructive means." The reason: "nothing diminishes the number of wars so effectively."[7]

There is an unforgettable exposition of this view in fiction, to which I should like to devote a little space. In *War and Peace* Tolstoy has a discussion between the soldier Prince Andrei Bolkonsky and the civilian Pierre Bezuhov in Bolkonsky's tent on the eve of the Battle of Borodino.[8] The conversation begins with Andrei's criticism of the German general Barclay de Tolly, who had until recently been in charge of the Russian forces

7. Quoted in James T. Johnson, *Just War Tradition and the Restraint of War* (Princeton University Press, 1981), p. 301.

8. Tolstoy, *War and Peace,* tr. Rosemary Edmonds (Penguin Books, 1957), bk. 3, pt. 2, ch. 25.

against Napoleon. Barclay had conducted the campaign strictly according to the laws of war. In retreating before the French he had forbidden his troops to pillage the country; and at Smolensk he had refused to engage Napoleon because he was outnumbered. "He could not understand," says Andrei, "that for the first time we were fighting on Russian soil, that there was a spirit in the men such as I had never seen before."

"They say he's an able general, though," remarked Pierre. "I don't know what is meant by 'an able general,'" replied Prince Andrei ironically. "An able general," said Pierre, "well, it's one who leaves nothing to chance . . . who foresees the adversary's intentions." "But that's impossible!" cried Prince Andrei . . . "The relative strength of opposing armies can never be predicted. You may be quite sure," he went on, "that if things depended on arrangements made by the staff, I should be there helping to make those arrangements . . . Success never has and never will depend on position, on equipment, or even on numbers—least of all on position." "What does it depend on, then?" "On the feeling that is in me and in him . . . and in every soldier . . . A battle is won by the side that is firmly resolved to win . . . The side that fights the more savagely and spares itself least will win."

The discussion now takes a new turn, as Andrei outlines his philosophy for the transformation of war:

"One thing I would do if I had the power," he began again. "I would not take prisoners. What sense is there in taking prisoners? It's playing knights of old. The French have destroyed my home and are on their way to destroy Moscow; they have outraged and are out-raging me every moment. They are my enemies. In my opinion they are all criminals . . . They must be put to death . . . Not to take prisoners," Prince Andrei con-tinued. "That by itself would transform the whole aspect of war and make it less cruel. As it is we have been playing at war—that's what's vile! . . . They prate about the rules of warfare, of chivalry, of flags of truce and humanity to the wounded, and so on. All fiddle-sticks . . . No quarter, I say, but kill and be killed! . . . If there were none of this magnanimity business in war-fare, we should never go to war except for something worth facing certain death for, as now. There would not be wars because Paul Ivanich had given offence to Mihail Ivanich. And when there was a war, like this present one, it would be war! And then the spirit and determination of the fighting men would be some-thing quite different . . . War is not a polite recreation but the vilest thing in life, and we ought to understand that and not play at war . . . Let war be war and not a game . . . The aim and end of war is murder; the weap-ons employed in war are espionage, treachery and the encouragement of treachery, the ruining of a country, the plundering and robbing of its inhabitants for the maintenance of the army, and tricking and lying which all appear under the heading of the art of war."

This masterful exposition of the nineteenth-centu-ry conception of total war has two main elements: a criticism and a proposal. In the first place it criticises the traditional attempt to impose constraints of reason and order upon the conduct of war. This criticism is directed at several objects at once: at the pretensions of strategists to devise a "scientific" art of war; at the

protocol of the professional military establishment
which makes a career out of war; and, without distinguishing them from these purely professional conventions, the moral restraints with which just-war theory
had surrounded the conduct of war, such as the duty
to take and protect prisoners of war, the prohibition of
marauding, and the requirement that no engagement
should be entered without reasonable hope of success.
These elements of military culture are treated indiffer-
ently by Prince Andrei and wrapped in an all-embrac-
ing blanket of suspicion. They indicate the "Germanic"
drive to be rational where rationality is out of place;
they obscure the untamed reality of war with the formal appearance of rational control. In place of reason
Andrei appeals to "feeling", the emotional commitment, in this case to defend Russian soil, which alone
can ensure success. This "feeling", when given free
rein, is the source of the "resolve to win"; and this in
turn produces the "savagery" and readiness for sacrifice that are the immediate preconditions for victory.
Such is Andrei's art of war. War is to be won by letting
loose unrestrained and non-rational forces in the
human spirit. The good generals in *War and Peace*, and
especially Kutuzov, are those who plan little, interfere
little, and simply allow the spirit of the men to work
itself out unhindered.

The second element is the proposal for the deterrence of war. By allowing all war to be total war, free
of the constraints that have hitherto inhibited it, we
will, according to Andrei's argument, impose a moral
limit on the inception of war. Only those causes
which are capable of exciting this passionate popular

feeling will be justified causes of war. Furthermore, we will at the same time impose a prudential limit. By allowing war to proceed with all the savagery of which it is capable, we will provide the most effective disincentive to trivial recourse to war. Andrei is not a moral cynic. He is attempting simply to re-focus the moral question away from the *ius in bello* to the *ius ad bellum*. He is the antecedent of all those twentieth-century thinkers who have argued that the principal, or only, crime in war is to begin it for insufficient reason.

There is an ambiguity in the way Andrei states his case which throws important light upon the presuppositions from which he works. On the one hand he is proposing a self-conscious enhancement of the barbarity of war by refusing all quarter to surrendered prisoners. On the other hand he claims to be doing no more than expose what war really is, stripping away hypocritical pretense. "Let war be war!" he urges. But that presumes that he knows, and that we know, what war "really" is; that we know, in fact, that it consists of the evils which he catalogues, most of which had been treated by traditional moral thought as barbarous deformations of the practice of war which soldiers had been urged by all means to avoid. Andrei works, then, with a conception of war as "the vilest thing in life", and defends the project of making it viler than it need be by claiming to make its underlying essence explicit. Where does this doctrine of the essence of war come from? I can only conjecture; but conjecture I will, pointing to three different philosophical and theological sources of inspiration, all of which seem to have been influentially present in the minds of mid-nineteenth-century thinkers.

The first, once again, is the waning but still powerful seventeenth-century contractarian tradition. Hobbes had given currency to the idea that the state of war and the state of nature were one and the same thing, and although Locke had protested against this, his objection was only to the idea that the state of nature necessarily implied war, not to the idea that war implied the state of nature.[9] War thus came to be conceived, as a matter of definition, as the absence at least of all political order, if not as the absence of all order whatsoever. But this was a purely definitional matter, not the result of any analysis of warfare in actuality, a subject in which the dominant contractarian thinkers had no interest. Their predecessors, the late scholastic theologians of the Counter-Reformation, had understood war quite differently, not as the *absence* of political order but as the *last resort* of political order when the resources for judicial arbitration were not available. Thus for Suarez war was justified when "an act of punitive justice has proved indispensable to mankind and no more fitting method for its performance could be found."[10] The difference between these two views is of enormous moment: for the scholastics war is always an imperfect striving for international justice in unfavourable circumstances

9. Thomas Hobbes, *Leviathan,* ch. 13; John Locke, *Second Treatise on Goverment,* ch. 3. As with many contractarian ideas this was not original to Hobbes; Grotius was already arguing against unnamed advocates of the idea in 1625.

10. Suarez, *De caritate* XIII.4.

and essentially dependent upon notions of justice and order for its intelligibility, whereas for the contractarians war is the simple negation of justice and order. It is one of the miracles of Western thought that at the moment when contractarian political ideas overwhelmed the scholastic legacy, the central insight of the scholastics was preserved in the field of jurisprudence by the monumental figure of the Dutch jurist and theologian, Hugo Grotius. The subsequent history of just-war notions in law is well known, and acts as an important counter-balance to the nihilistic account of war which dominates the philosophical tradition.

A second source of Andrei's doctrine of the essence of war is the romantic understanding of history. The conception of an irrational historical necessity, which sweeps up men and nations in its course and defies all accounting, is present throughout *War and Peace*, especially in the long philosophical excursuses which daunt successive generations of Tolstoy's readers. Nobody, he tells us, was in control of the Franco-Prussian wars, certainly not either Napoleon or the Emperor Alexander. "A king is the slave of history. History, that is, the unconscious, universal swarm-life of mankind, uses every moment of the life of kings for its own purposes." Supremely it is war that represents the irruption of this irrational collective necessity into our various conscious purposes. "Millions of men, renouncing their human feelings and their common sense, had to march from West to East to slay their fellows, just as some centuries previously hordes of men had moved from East to West

slaying their fellows."[11] Tolstoy's own sceptical view
of the "swarm-life" is in contrast to Prince Andrei's
excitable enthusiasm for "the feeling which is in me
and in him . . . and in every soldier." But Andrei and
his creator are both acknowledging the same fundamentally irrational necessity as the force which
shapes all collective action and determines the course
of history, the passionate blindness of feeling which,
in one context or another, is constantly celebrated by
the romantic poets and thinkers of their century.

The third source to which I would point is the
nineteenth-century revival of ancient ideas about
warfare which we often refer to loosely as "Holy War",
ideas that are especially characteristic of the historical
narratives of the Old Testament surrounding the conquest of Canaan. The heart of the Holy War tradition
is that war is theophany. It is the irruption of divine
purposes into human activity: initiated by prophecy,
oracle, vision or divine possession and not by military
or political strategy, conducted not by self-directing
political agents but by human instruments who are
wielded like weapons in the hand of the Lord of hosts,
won not by superior numbers or by military discipline
but by miracle and by incalculable providential dispositions and stratagems. To this warfare its soldiers
are consecrated like religious acolytes, summoned to
perform the sacrifice faithfully and to observe the
divine self-disclosure. This last feature especially at-
tracted nineteenth-century imaginations, which
found the religious imagery potently suggestive of the

11. *War and Peace*, bk. 3, pt. 1, ch. 1.

commitment demanded by wars fought in the service of the highest ideals—our minds go at once to Julia Ward Howe's famous "Battle Hymn of the Republic": "Mine eyes have seen the glory of the coming of the Lord", written for the Federal cause in the American civil war. In Russia, where the theological role assigned to the Tsar always had a flavour of the Messianic about it, Holy War sentiments were naturally congenial. Elsewhere in *War and Peace* Tolstoy includes a lengthy prayer supposedly authorised by the Synod in 1812 which lays extensive claim upon the Holy War categories of the Old Testament: Russia is Jerusalem, its people Israel, and for Alexander are involved the victories of Moses over Amalek, Gideon over Midian, and David over Goliath.[12]

This religious background to the idea of total-war deterrence helps us to understand how deterrence is supposed to work. For although war is conceived as lying *beyond* the limits of the rational world, the hope is that if its presence can be made decisive enough it will ensure the perpetuation of peace and order *within* the rational world. The root of this hope is theophany. The appearing of the Lord of hosts at the head of his worshippers in battle overthrows all human designs and calculations, yet at the same time guarantees the security of human designs by the gracious bestowal of victory and peace. The theophanic hope is still discernible in those secular versions of the idea in which the forces of history assume the role of God.

But this helps us to formulate our principal theo-

12. Ibid., bk. 3, pt. 1, ch. 18.

logical objection. For the Holy War tradition is a hereti-
cal one in Christian thought, since, from the perspective of New Testament faith, the theophanic expectations which were built around war in the
conquest-narratives have been decisively transferred
to the death and resurrection of Christ. The form in
which divinity sweeps across our human undertakings to throw them to the ground and create them
anew is not war but the appearing of God in Jesus of
Nazareth. This is the significance which the evange-
lists, especially St. Luke, attribute to Jesus' rebuke to
Peter in the Garden of Gethsemane. From this central
theological objection we may derive two further critical comments. In the first place, human affairs, even
in war, cannot be the absolute expression of disorder
which the total-war idea conceives of. Since war is not
divine but creaturely, we can discern even in war the
vestiges of order and the striving for order. In the second place, the shape of history, if seen in the light of
the revelation of God in Jesus, cannot be determined
simply by the pointless marches of conquest, the irrational outpourings of violence and the paroxysms of
overwhelming collective feeling. Our objection, then,
takes on a trinitarian shape. The deterrence-idea tells
the truth neither about the Creator, nor about the
Messiah, nor about the Spirit. The Creator did not
make total disorder and set it abroad in war; the Messiah is not revealed in war; and the Spirit does not
direct history simply through irrational outbreaks of
mass violence.

The Strategic Era:
The Disclosure of War's Ultimate Form

Under the protection of the romantic historicism of the nineteenth century, then, the idea took root that it was the destiny of war to cancel itself out of history by vast increases in scale and violence which would result in the increasing prevalence of peace. This idea reached a turning point with the First World War. During the great pacifist reaction of the twenties and thirties of this century, it sprang to new life with the triumphant assertion that the long-awaited moment had come, the ultimate measure of war's destructiveness had been revealed, so that peace was now a necessity—if people would only recognise what they had seen and acknowledge its meaning.

> Some decades ago war may have been an instrument which, although it was brutal, could be used to resolve intolerable international tension; but today, owing to the fact that it cannot be controlled, it has lost even this shred of utility . . . War has outlived itself. It has become so colossal that it can no longer exercise any sensible function. To expect to establish a just order by means of a world conflagration—called war—has become political madness.[13]

I quote those words, written by Emil Brunner in 1932, simply because they are representative of a myriad of comparable assertions from the theologians, philosophers and pundits of every kind. They do not, of course, express classical Christian pacifism. To the or-

13. Emil Brunner, *The Divine Imperative*, tr. Olive Wyon (Westminster Press, 1947), pp. 470f.

thodox pacifist, I take it, it can be of no interest
whether war "today" is any different from war "some
decades ago", since they are both alike prohibited.
This is rather an attempt to extract pacifist conclusions
from an ostensible just-war foundation by arguing
from the disproportionate character of *modern* war, an
attempt which entirely depends on the historicist assumption that war has undergone a necessary quan-
titative and qualitative evolution. There is more than
a hint of Clausewitz's pronouncement that "real warfare" has made an "appearance . . . just in our own
times". The task remaining is purely pedagogical: to
force an acknowledgment that the evolution of war
has been universal, irreversible and necessary, that
this is how war now is, that it must ever be so, and has
always had the destiny within itself of becoming so.

Another development was taking place in the
same period; and the two developments, though superficially opposed, had a deep philosophical affinity.
That other development was the conception of the
strategic air-strike. The perfection of the aeroplane
had opened up possibilities of air-borne weapons, and
the deterrence-idea provided a context within which
this assumed great strategic importance. Advocates of
"strategic bombardment" urged that the use of air-
strikes against population-centres at the beginning of
a war would ensure the speediest surrender of the
enemy and the cessation of hostilities almost before
they had begun.[14] Once again technology seemed to
offer that enhancement of the disproportion between

14. See Lawrence Freedman, *The Evolution of Nuclear
Strategy* (Macmillan, 1981), pp. 3-21.

armed force and the will to resist which would make resistance arbitrary. These expectations for aerial bombing were based not on an assessment of the material damage it was likely to do to life and property, but on the expected effect upon civilian morale. It seemed to promise, in other words, that war could be won without having to be fought, since the enemy could be persuaded from the beginning that resistance was pointless. It is in this context that the word "strategic" acquired its distinctive twentieth-century meaning, referring not to the activities of generals but to the threats of international politics. The price, however, for allowing military strategy to convert itself into a method of not fighting wars was that international politics thereafter became reconceived on pseudo-military lines.

The historicist pacifists of the period, then, hailed the Great War as the war that would end all wars, while the early strategic theorists hailed aerial bombardment as the military technique that would end all wars. Common to both was the idea that the evolving disproportion of war would necessarily banish war from human affairs, and the resolve to make use of this disproportion in order to achieve that end. The one group used it as a strategy of *argument* merely, the other as a strategy of *action* which required continued efforts towards the technological enhancement of war. The advent of nuclear arms, finally, at the end of the Second World War, was necessitated by the strategy of action and welcome to the strategy of argument.

For the pacifists the claims made for nuclear warfare were more or less the same as those made for the

Great War. Each in its turn represented the great disclosure of the essence of war and of its inherent tendency to categorical disproportion. Some words of Karl Barth put these claims at their clearest:

> Much is already gained if only we do at last soberly admit that, whatever may be the purpose or possible justice of a war, it now means that without disguise or shame, not only individuals or even armies, but whole nations as such are out to destroy one another by every possible means. It only needed the atom and hydrogen bomb to complete the self-disclosure of war in this regard.[15]

But for the strategy of action the claims now reached a new pitch, as though the practical deterrentists at last became convinced that they could now substantiate what the theoretical deterrentists had said was the case. At this point we find it said that weapons have been designed without the intention of their being used, and that the purpose of the strategic force is not to reduce the frequency of resort to war or to bring wars to an end almost as soon as they start, but to prevent them from ever occurring. With these claims the idea of deterrence reaches its full maturity. Mankind now thinks himself in a position to promise, on the basis of an absolute disproportion of force to the political good, the abolition of war.

It may well seem curious, this intertwining of pacifist goals and total-war strategy which makes up the deterrence-idea, so curious, indeed, that the inter-

15. Karl Barth, *Church Dogmatics* III/4, tr. G. W. Bromily, T. F. Torrance, et al. (T. & T. Clark, 1961), p. 149.

pretation we have put forward may meet with dis-
belief, and that despite the daily evidence of our ears.
For it is not from pacifists alone that we hear the les-
son recited that there is no winning of a nuclear war,
that it is folly to think of fighting one. And it is not the
ostensible defenders of deterrence alone who affirm
that nuclear weapons are potent "to warn sinful and
stupid humanity away from all war as a means of set-
tling international disputes."[16] To judge by what we
hear, the debate could seem to turn on only one question: whether it is necessary actually to *possess* nuclear
weapons to achieve perpetual peace or whether it is
sufficient, and quite as effective, merely to *think* about
them! Yet conscientious and sometimes even intel-
ligent commentators continue to represent the great
disagreement of our time as though it were a classical
confrontation between realists and idealists, between
Creon and Antigone.[17] Why? Partly because we underestimate the tenacity of nineteenth-century his-

16. *The Church and the Bomb,* Report of a Working Party of
the Church of England Board for Social Responsibility
(Church Information Office, 1982), p. 149.

17. I allude to the title of a paper by D. M. MacKinnon,
which follows this line of analysis which I think must ulti-
mately be fruitless. MacKinnon does, however, touch on the
heart of the matter when he writes: "What I would plead for
is that we recognise the sheer magnitude of the changes that
have been allowed to take place . . . For these changes are, in
the forms in which we have received them, a perverted practical expression of the radically transformed understanding of
the world in which we live . . ." (*Themes in Theology* [T. & T.
Clark, 1987], p. 130).

toricism, so often debunked by philosophical revolutions and yet so persistent in the common mind, with its cargo of millenarian expectations and utopian hopes. The ambivalence which we feel to this legacy of world-historical self-confidence must go some way to explain our difficulty in discussing it clearly. But there is another factor. The deterrence-idea generated predictions which have since been disproved by events, and the apparently clearly-drawn lines of our current debate conceal a scramble for fresh positions. It is to this failure that we turn next.

CHAPTER III

Failure

THE DETERRENCE-IDEA brought the nuclear age into being, and came to maturity with it as a programme for "massive retaliation" in the event of an enemy attack. Some words of John Foster Dulles, American Secretary of State in the fifties, summarise the idea in the form which was characteristic of the decade after Hiroshima. "The heart of the problem is how to deter attack. This, we believe, requires that a potential aggressor be left in no doubt that he would be certain to suffer damage outweighing any possible gains from aggression."[1] Three remarks may serve as a commentary upon Dulles's programme.

"The heart of the problem", in the first place, was "to deter attack". We observe at once how narrowly defined this problematic is. There are many other objectives that a state might normally be expected to pursue in its self-interested dealings with other states: more favourable access to the world's markets

1. Quoted in Lawrence Freedman, *The Evolution of Nuclear Strategy* (Macmillan, 1981), p. 87.

55

and resources, the establishment of friendly regimes in neighbouring territories, rights of passage and abode for its nationals abroad, and security of travel in international waters. Even if we bracket out the self-interest, and ask only about the *just* objectives of international politics, we can compile a long list: the punishment and control of international terrorism and the suppression of piracy, the promotion of fairer markets, the encouragement of regimes which favour liberty and enforce their citizens' rights, the improvement of judicial and deliberative international institutions, and many others. Suppose, then, we excuse the narrow objective on the grounds that it is, after all, appropriate for *military* pursuit? Even so, deterring attack is only a thread in the fabric of military—as of political—purposes, and hardly the most striking one at that. Military objectives include repelling attack when it comes, destroying the enemy's power to attack further, and establishing such effective control over governable and defensible territory that it will be possible to end hostilities and not merely to keep them at bay.

How, then, did this limited moment in the practice of war become the dominant purpose of international politics in peace? It happened because the overriding question which shaped the geopolitical aims of the major powers emerging from the Second World War was how war might be avoided in future. Not, that is, how the conditions for a just and stable peace might be sustained, but simply how war might be prevented. To the asking and answering of this question three traditions of political reasoning contributed: pacifism provided the end, the traditions of diplomacy and military strategy the means. But the wisdom which belonged to each of these traditions was cut short by their involvement with each other. Traditional pacifism would never have thought that threat and armed manoeuvre were apt means for its moral end. Diplomacy would never have thought the avoidance of war a sufficient goal for political pursuit, and neither did strategists use to consider the avoidance of war as fitting an end as the winning of it. The deterrence-idea drew selectively from these traditions without learning the practical and moral wisdom that each had to teach, driven on by the obsessive war-weariness of mid-century Europe.

Dulles argued in the second place that the potential aggressor should be left "in no doubt". As Lawrence Freedman observes, "the policy attempted to introduce a certainty into adversary calculations."[2] The succeeding generation of statesmen, who forged the still current NATO policy of Flexible Response in the 1960's, were no less concerned than Dulles to introduce certainty into the calculations of the Warsaw Pact leaders, even though their hope was now to achieve this end by leaving everything *uncertain* about the purposes of the West. "The incalculability of the risk impresses upon the potential aggressor that an attack cannot be a rational option"[3]—which is to say that by making oneself incalculable one makes one's adver-

2. Ibid.

3. Robert Osgood and Henning Wegener, *Deterrence: the Western Approach* (NATO Information Service, 1986), p. 5.

sary calculable. This kind of certainty, however, is not to be had when human actions and reactions are in question. In this respect, too, we can see deterrence as a "technological" idea, attempting to make the free interaction of peoples conformable to mechanical standards of predictability. In this respect, too, it betrays its Hobbesian roots, striving to focus attention upon the moment when human reason, shorn of its customary complexity and wealth of motivation, is bound to produce action of one kind and of one kind only. If absolute security against war is to be achieved, something of the mechanical must come to characterise our expectations of one another.

In the third place we notice the means adopted to this end, which is to threaten "damage outweighing any possible gains from aggression". The key-word is "possible". That word makes the difference between deterrence as the modern age has thought it and the traditional threat of retaliation which has always accompanied defence against attack. Where traditional threats of retaliation have matched the aggressor step by step, depriving him of all actual gains of actual aggression—and, of course, throwing in something extra to reward him for his pains—modern deterrence reaches out as though to touch an imaginary boundary, depriving him, in anticipatory warning, of all *possible* gains of any *possible* aggression. Its character, as I have argued above, is the resort to disproportion; and its logic is to make disproportion ultimate, so that it will outweigh "any possible gains" and not only those gains which the adversary may conceivably think to lie within his grasp.

Ultimate Disproportion

We must explore a little further the notion of an "ultimate" or "categorical" disproportion. To describe the nuclear deterrent in these terms is not, of course, to pass judgment on its status as a technical achievement; our experience suggests, indeed, that no weapon can be ultimate in the sense that it cannot be superseded by further technical improvement. The nuclear deterrent is ultimate simply by being posited as such. The deterrence-idea requires a deterrent that will be like the Anselmic definition of God: that than which no greater can be thought. Only so can it pretend to wield the instrument of disproportion in such a way as to constrain any *possible* adventure of human aggressiveness.

Here I risk being told that I have chosen altogether too crude a version of deterrence-theory as material for my analysis. Even if the idea of an "ultimate" disproportion did lie behind the earlier doctrinal thinking of the Western alliance, ought we not to admit that with Flexible Response a less totalitarian ambition has prevailed? Here, it would seem, the whole point is *not* to reach for a supposed *ne plus ultra*, a boundary-line which can be possessed in advance of enemy intentions, but simply to match aggression with reprisal step by step *ad infinitum*. Advocates of this distinction are likely to urge that "ultimate" disproportion is anyway an elusive and unusable concept. Something is disproportionate or proportionate *relatively to* something else. In the 1920's pacifists argued that modern war had outgrown all usefulness; in the 1930's the sight of the Nazi Reich encouraged many of them to rediscover a use for it. Is it not always the case, then, that proportion or disproportion depends upon the scale of the threat which has to be met, and that no outer limit can be set to the scope of proportionate response until an outer limit is set to the scope of wrongdoing itself? By this argument defenders of Flexible Response claim that NATO policy can observe "the law of proportionality between attack and defensive action" even up to the level of a general nuclear war.[4]

But proportion in the deployment of armed force is relative not only to the scale of the particular attack that provokes it, but to the political good of human communities as a whole. There are fixed limits of human mortality and of possible cultural survival; and it is from these limits that the idea of an "ultimate" disproportion derives its meaning. It refers to a measure of force that will frustrate any conceivable political goods that either defender or attacker may think to achieve or protect. It has, in fact, often been acknowledged by strategic thinkers that there comes a point at which further increment in destructive power is simply irrelevant to political goals. "What in the name of God is strategic superiority?" Henry Kissinger once famously exclaimed. "What is the significance of it politically, militarily, operationally, at these levels of numbers? What do you do with it?"[5] Those who first articulated the mature philosophy of deterrence believed that the possession of this point of vantage, from which all human endeavours could be rendered

4. Ibid., p. 11.
5. Quoted in Freedman, *Evolution of Nuclear Strategy*, p. 363.

nugatory, would give them the political control over their enemies' undertakings that they sought. And even in its redesigned form deterrence-theory cannot dispense with that belief. The dissuasive weight that is reposed upon the incalculable risk of resort to a general nuclear war is simply another way of possessing this same point of vantage. To call this resort "proportional" is to abstract the measure of proportion from all reference to human purposes and to reduce it to a mere equilibration of megatons.

Deterrence, then, has not got away from the pursuit of ultimate disproportion, nor is that pursuit in itself inherently nonsensical. It is merely breathtakingly bold. To undertake to harness ultimate disproportion to secure proximate political goals can only be described, from a religious point of view, as "impiety". And as such it draws its own nemesis with it. At the climax of John of Patmos's great series of political visions we meet the spectacle of a whore that has presumed to ride on the back of a beast. The whore, for John as for the prophets whose imagery he borrowed, is an empire—just another empire like the Babylon whose name she bears. The beast, on the other hand, is something new in history, the Antichrist summoned from the abyss to challenge God's Messiah and his reign. As for the alliance between the whore and the beast: from one point of view, we might say, it is a nice ride, and from the other a nice meal![6] To employ su-

6. Revelation 17. For a fuller account of John of Patmos see my lecture "The Political Thought of the Book of Revelation", *Tyndale Bulletin* xxxvii (1986), pp. 61-94.

perhuman powers as an instrument of political control is to be absorbed into their hostility towards God and towards human welfare. The history of the deterrence-idea since the Second World War has been the story of how the political ambitions which promoted it have been swallowed up by the means they sought to use.

Elements of Failure

The phrase "when deterrence fails" is often used as a euphemism for the eventuality of nuclear war; but it would be more judicious if the failure of deterrence were spoken of not as a possible future contingency but as an accomplished fact. Deterrence is a pattern of thought. It is a posture of practical reason which bases itself upon a claim to discern certain realities about the way nations act and react, and this claim is open to the usual tests of adequacy when measured against experience.[7] What has occurred since the first decade of nuclear deterrence has been the unravelling of what began as a tight conception of international management, through a series of failed predictions and unforeseen developments, into a string of forced adaptations to reality.

This failure has been analysed many times and in

7. Cf. Robin Gill, *The Cross against the Bomb* (Epworth, 1984), p. 1: "It is not a fact that nuclear weapons have prevented a European war since 1945. It is a theory, which one may seek to justify or discount."

many ways. I shall trace it from what I take to be its central mistake, in five steps:

1. Deterrence proposed to create a *practical self-evidence* about the folly of war. Its primary purpose was epistemological. Everyone had to be made to understand that recourse to war was madness. In order to create this transparent self-evidence, it turned to technologically enhanced threats; but that was where it was bound to fail. No combination of armaments and threatenings could ever effect a transparency of motive and intention, so as to remove all suspicion and doubt. Despite every attempt to make things clear, nations in the deterrence era are as much as ever prey to uncertainty. In its attempt to remove elements of ambiguity which cannot be removed, the deterrence-idea betrayed its affinity with the idealist philosophies of the nineteenth century.

There is abiding uncertainty, in the first place, about whether the would-be deterrer will actually use the sanctions that he threatens. For deterrence to be credible, the weapon must be usable; but it was designed precisely to be unusable. The deterrer is a political agent, guided by his own rational political ends. There is, therefore, an intrinsic incredibility about his threat, which it could serve no rational political end to carry out. As we have observed, some theorists hope to turn this element of uncertainty to good effect, pleading that even the remote possibility of use will ensure a practical certainty in the adversary's calculations. But this is unhistorical thinking. Remote possibilities may deter initially, but not for ever. Political pressures drive nations to test the limits of their freedom, and in the end it is inevitable that the incredible threat will be tested by some adversary who does not believe it.

This line of thought has frequently led strategic thinkers back to the consideration of automatic reprisal systems such as the launch-on-warning programme. The virtue of these, from the point of view of the theorist, is that they remove the element of doubt which the presence of rational human decision-makers creates. We are reminded of Prince Andrei's contention that in warmaking one ought to abandon rational calculation and entrust oneself to blind feeling. The technological equivalent of blind feeling is automation. The enemy must know, runs the argument, that if he goes beyond a certain point no reasonable doubts on our side can protect him from reprisals. Only so will deterrence deter. Automation embodies pure will, dissociated from the humanity of political reason. It expresses the radically voluntarist character of deterrence, the hope to prevent war by pure resolve liberated from the determination of practical rational ends.[8]

2. If there is doubt about the behaviour of the deterrer, there is equal doubt about the behaviour of the

8. Cf. Paul Ramsey, *The Just War* (Scribners, 1968), p. 222: "In war as a trial of wills, what one side does is determined primarily by its calculation of what the other side expects of it, or what is required for its resolution to be broken. Analysts in our day have developed an entire science of purely voluntaristic games of strategy simply by abstracting the encounter of the wills and minds of the combatants from the other factors."

party to be deterred. Lawrence Freedman identifies this as the "central problem" in deterrence theory: "the transgressor maintains options other than full compliance."[9] The purpose was to put the transgressor in a position where, as a rational agent, he could do only one thing; but such a degree of predictability is not achievable. In order to make it look more plausible, the deterrence-idea borrowed from contractarian sources a conception of human rationality which supposed that in the right circumstances it would respond to one motive only, the fear of extinction. The artificiality of this supposition now becomes apparent; for in fact we have not succeeded in programming our enemies' behaviour and we still do not know how they will respond to our threats.

This uncertainty produces one very striking result. It gives the deterrer almost as great an interest as his enemy in ensuring that the effectiveness of deterrence is never put to the test. The price he pays for deterring the wrongdoer from wrongdoing is that he deters himself from wrongdoing, too—but according to *his enemy's* idea of wrongdoing, not his. He accepts the loss of his freedom to pursue legitimate political objectives (as he sees them) if the enemy, however unreasonably, would perceive them as threatening his interests. So the concept of deterrence as an instrument of justice, securing the world against anarchic breaches of international order, quickly breaks down into the moral indifferentism of "mutual" deterrence. In the fifties and sixties the Americans did not oppose Soviet ambitions

9. Freedman, *Evolution of Nuclear Strategy,* p. 88.

in the field of nuclear arms; and that was because the farsighted among them understood that deterrence must of its nature tend towards mutuality, and they hoped that if this became explicit it would contribute to stability. Indeed, the real logic of deterrence points irresistibly in the direction of what we still deplore as "proliferation"—the possession of a deterrent by every major power. To see this is to see the moral scepticism which gave rise to the deterrence-idea, and to abandon the notion that deterrence can be effective in the service of international justice. On the contrary, it must enhance the autonomy and anarchic independence of nations, making the task of just arbitration in international disputes infinitely more difficult.

3. But even the promised *stability* of mutual deterrence proved illusory. The point of deterrence, we recall, was not to prevent *nuclear* war, but to prevent *any* war or warlike aggression. If the sole purpose had been to avoid nuclear war, it could have been achieved quite simply by one side's laying down its nuclear arms and submitting to whatever purposes the other had in mind for it. But the point was to prevent *aggression,* by making war—all war—unthinkable as a tool of policy. But war has not been made unthinkable. It continues to be thought, and, indeed, practised. When apologists for deterrence boast that Europe has been kept free of war for forty years, we are entitled to ask to what battlefields outside of Europe the two superpowers have exported their conflict. Vietnam, Afghanistan, Korea—all scenes of local conflict in the first instance, to be sure—have become the surrogates for Berlin and Vienna.

The words "stable balance of terror" attempt to define a mathematical point without dimensions. If the balance is *stable*, then the possibility arises that one side may venture upon a small military enterprise, convinced that the other will be deterred from escalating it. Stability at the nuclear level creates instability at the sub-nuclear level. The "nuclear umbrella" makes life safe not merely for a breathless, motionless peace but for a certain amount of traditional rough and tumble, the very kind of thing that it was supposed to ensure against. If, on the other hand, the stability is maintained by a balance *of terror,* then we have always to be looking over the abyss and contemplating the prospect that the balance may break down. And as soon as that danger becomes a factor, it provokes a desperate scramble for the safety of a superior position. A historian of deterrence has commented on "the cyclical character" of the strategic debates since the end of the Second World War.[10] That cyclical pattern arises from the inevitable oscillation which occurs around the mathematical point without dimensions: on the one hand an emphasis on stability, built on the massive destructive potential of strategic missiles directed at population-centres, on the other hand an emphasis on the balance of terror, in which warfighting plans based on intermediate-range and battlefield weapons are directed to achieving victory in limited nuclear conflict. At one pole of the cycle we have local wars, at the other we have confrontations in which we seem poised on the brink.

10. Freedman, p. xv.

At neither pole is there the true stability of a well-founded peace.

That is to say, the deterrent state is continually having its bluff called. It is forced into positions where it must show something like a definite intention to fight a nuclear war if it is to keep deterrence credible. Deterrence, of course, is not a policy of bluff. The bluffing state (as it appears in theoretical discussion; such a thing could hardly exist in reality) is supposed to have made up its mind that if the deterrence-project fails, it will not carry out its threats. The deterrent state has not formed any such intention, but has left the question open to be decided on the day. While the day is distant it can comfortably be assumed that the decision for nuclear war is "unthinkable". But as the day approaches, as it does in moments of heightened crisis, the absence of any decisive plan for action "on the day" leaves a vacuum into which the hypothetical plan of nuclear attack is inevitably drawn. By degrees the hypothetical intention becomes the actual intention, since it is the only intention that the state has formed for the occasion and it can hardly renounce it while it is still hoping to squeeze the last possible ounce of deterrence-effect from it. The logic of deterrence itself, which forbids it ever to cease trying to deter, even after the war has begun, requires the deterrent state to actuate its hypothetical plan and undertake what everyone used to know could not possibly be undertaken. The moment at which it is free to decide "on the day" never comes; the path leads without a break from deterrence on the brink of war to deterrence in the midst of war. Thus it happens that the deterrent designed to be unusable in war becomes the means contemplated for use in war.

4. This brings us to the most striking feature of the deterrence-age, which according to the published prospectus should never have happened: the arms race. In explaining why the pioneers of deterrence-thinking never foresaw this result of their policies, we have to observe that the idea suffered from the beginning from a naiveté about technology, a legacy from the idealist philosophy which inspired it. Idealism fostered contradictory notions about means and ends. On the one hand it continued to speak about means and ends in a classical way, supposing that means were shaped and directed to serve ends that were conceived before them. On the other hand it introduced the notion of an ultimate end of human history. But an ultimate end, situated at the horizon of history, does not function in the same way as a proximate end in relation to the means that are adopted to achieve it. It confers infinite legitimation upon the means without imposing a corresponding formal discipline. As a result the means become autonomous; and here is born one important feature of modern technology, which Jacques Ellul has characterised as "the ensemble of means" in a civilisation where "the means are more important than the ends".[11] But autonomous means can never effect a stable end. The end recedes indefinitely over the horizon, while the continual enhancement of the means becomes its own proximate

11. Jacques Ellul, *The Technological Society*, tr. J. Wilkinson (Random House, 1964), p. 19.

end, uncontrolled by any clear vision of what is to be achieved by it. Progress in technique refuses to yield a deterrent which is genuinely "ultimate" in the sense that the theory requires. In that there is always more technical progress, the formal end of a stable peace never arrives, since anxiety over the next development always pre-empts it. So the whole content of deterrence has become something different from what was first announced as "the stable balance of terror". It has become a breathless race to stand still. Deterrence is maintained only as either party strives unremittingly to keep up. Stability itself—genuine stability, that is, which would set us free to concentrate on other things—would, in the circumstances of deterrence, be destabilising.

5. A peculiar role in deterrence-by-arms-race is played by *measures aimed at securing defence,* and by measures directed against the enemy's weapons-systems rather than against his population. These measures characteristically speed up the arms-race. This fact was discovered rather painfully in 1962 as a result of Secretary Macnamara's famous attempt to redirect American missiles onto military rather than civilian targets, an enlightened measure, as it seemed, which was in keeping with the spirit of the just-war requirement of discriminate attack.[12] But it was interpreted by Soviet leaders as an attempt to achieve "first-strike capability", that is to say, the ability to neutralise the

12. On Macnamara's Ann Arbor speech and its consequences see Freedman, *Evolution of Nuclear Strategy,* pp. 234-44; also Ramsey, *Just War,* pp. 211-13.

enemy's deterrent in one strike, leaving him entirely vulnerable. Thus the new paradoxical rules of deterrence-by-arms-race announced themselves. Civilian targets are less provocative than military targets; defensive capability is more destabilising than capability for attack. These paradoxes about stability and destabilisation are now an established feature of all academic discourse on deterrence, deployed, one suspects, with an element of sheer *bravura* by those whose professional business it is to discuss these questions in public.

The paradox that defence is more destabilising than offence arises from the transference of military concepts to international relations. "Defence" is a word that is used analogously both of military and of political postures. To counsel a general at the inception of a campaign that all his battles should be fought in defensive positions would be ruinous; indeed, it would probably prevent the campaign from ever being brought to an end. But to counsel a statesman that he should never contemplate war for other reasons than defence against aggression is a different matter. Provided that "defence" was interpreted reasonably generously, the advice would be sound. Deterrence, by conceiving relations between states technologically, has taught us to discuss them as though they were extensions of battle. That is how we end up by telling our politicians, contrary to all our moral intuitions, to keep on the offensive. But political relations are not military strategies; the terms of the discussion are misconceived. Those who profess to oppose deterrence should not pay it the compliment of taking the strategic paradoxes upon their lips as though their wisdom were unchallengeable.

However, those who are committed to *maintaining* deterrence cannot ignore the validity of the paradoxes as ground-rules which determine the meaning of their actions within the context to which they have committed themselves. To take one obvious example: the Strategic Defence Initiative can mean only one thing *within the deterrence context,* and that is an intensive fuelling of the arms-race. The goal that President Reagan set himself in his famous speech in 1983 was to develop a defensive capability which could exist alongside offensive deterrence until it was so totally secure that deterrence could safely be dismantled.[13] Leaving on one side the question of whether this is technically possible, a matter on which I am not qualified to hold a view, it makes no sense to think that those with a continuing interest in maintaining offensive deterrence (i.e., the NATO allies) could sit still and allow their own defensive technology to overtake them. Why should the allies deny themselves the advantage of using information gained from their work on defensive systems to improve their offensive systems? And if defensive systems continue to feed improvements into offensive systems, how can the day ever come when the offensive systems have been rendered permanently ineffective by the defensive systems? The implication of the S.D.I. programme is a

13. For the text of President Reagan's address see *Weapons in Space,* ed. F. A. Long, D. Hafner, and J. Boutwell (Norton, 1986), pp. 351-53.

curious one: the West, not content with an arms-race against the Soviet Union, has entered a yet more hectic arms-race against itself!

To escape this implication it would be necessary for any power which proposed to develop defensive systems to withdraw simultaneously from its offensive deterrence-posture; for otherwise that posture must dictate how the new move is understood. But we must not assume as a matter of course that defensive weapons-systems would be the best way out of the impasse of failed deterrence. Such an assumption springs precisely from the same confusion between military and political senses of "defence" which deterrence has encouraged. There is nothing morally superior about defensive *weapons*. The moral problem is not that the weapons are offensive, but that they are designed to carry out attacks which could have no rational or moral purpose. It is the defensive *cause* which the moral presumption must favour, and its prosecution by rational and just hostilities, whether offensively or defensively sustained.

Will and Belief

Now let us stand back and review the unravelling of the deterrence-idea which forty years of experience have effected. We must comment in the first place upon the *goal* which deterrence set itself, and which links it with classical pacifism, the total avoidance of war. War is the only forum of international justice that most ages have known. If war is to become a thing of the past, it must surely be through new institutions which can offer aggrieved nations a reasonable and reliable hope of justice in their disputes with other nations. If, as Suarez said, war is justified when "an act of punitive justice has proved indispensable to mankind, and no more fitting method for its performance could be found", then the work we have in hand is to find more fitting methods, by creating and improving tribunals that can judge between nations. The abolition of war *in this sense*—that is, the transmuting of bilateral conflict into authoritative and impartial arbitration—is a worthy goal for humanity. What deterrence has tried to do is to block the resort to war without satisfying the need of justice which provokes it. Incidentally it has also frustrated attempts to establish dispassionate arbitration of international causes; how this is so we shall see more fully as we proceed.

We may comment next upon the *means* by which deterrence hoped to achieve its end: rendering the behaviour of nations predictable. It did not succeed in doing this; but it did, by evoking a belief in its own power to predict human behaviour, secure a limited conformity with its predictions. The two major global powers have tended to act up to the expectations which the theory of deterrence has had of them, partly because they believe it, and partly because it suits them that there should be a certain mutual predictability, so that the predictions of deterrence provide a set of conventions which each side tacitly agrees to follow. Deterrence, therefore, forms a closed circle of interpretation and action within which it is currently convenient to manage inter-bloc relations. It controls our behaviour by our belief in it, a belief in which questions of truth and usefulness are not distinguished. But because deterrence offers itself as a universal doctrine and demands of us a commitment *ad infinitum*, we fail to see that the conventions of deterrence cannot possibly sustain themselves. The arms-race is too expensive, even for the superpowers; and the new nuclear powers, as they arise, will have less interest in maintaining long-term stability. When we are told, then, that deterrence is stable, we are told it because the more we believe it the better the prospects for stability become. That is to say, the stability it pretends to offer is not grounded in the reality of things, but is self-conjured out of a dialectic of will and belief. But when belief in any thing is not exacted from us as the tribute due to the self-evidence of reality but is begged from us as a service to the common good, we know that we have to do with a threadbare ideology. The circularity of such belief must finally earn it contempt, even if for the moment it strikes everyone as witty and clever. When we see someone poised in mid-air without visible means of support, we applaud; but we know that, however the trick is done, he will not be there for very long.

The question has often been asked in Western culture: can sheer self-confidence evoke enough belief to conjure social reality out of nothing? Before the sociologists began theorising about the question, the story-tellers were dividing on it. The Brothers Grimm ("The Brave Little Tailor") answered Yes; Hans Christian Andersen ("The Emperor's New Clothes") answered No. For the theologian the question is posed, and answered, in its decisive form by St. John of Patmos. The character of contemporary political life as he saw it was that of a sustained parody of social order. The Antichrist commanded an organised and disciplined human society, a market for trade, a social philosophy; and all on the strength of the sheer belief which the worshipping masses reposed in him. But this order, lacking foundation in reality, had to collapse in on itself. The client kings who derived their authority from the empire of the beast had to turn against it and destroy it.[14] This, surely, must be the fate of the deterrent state. Lacking foundation in reality for managing its international relations the way it does, it must collapse. The only thing we do not know, and which may yet be undetermined, is whether it will collapse in mere ridicule, as in Hans Christian Andersen's genial tale, or in massive geopolitical and ecological disaster.

14. Revelation 17:16.

CHAPTER IV

Intention

THE ORDER of international peace is founded on the minimal recognition of one society by another. Not, that is, on the recognition of one *government* by another, which is merely a conventional device to ensure and facilitate communication among nations; but on the recognition by each society that the other human societies which dwell upon the earth have a right to do so, and that this right needs to be respected even in the course of open hostilities. So it was that the traditional principles of justice in war required that only the enemy's forces, and not his population, should be subject to direct attack. This was a way of saying, with Augustine: "even in making war, you must be a peacemaker."[1] Nothing could justify an attempt to wipe another people off the face of the earth. In its classical form just-war theory expressed this principle of discrimination individualistically, as a matter of distinguishing between the innocent and guilty members of the enemy society. This formula-

1. *Epistulae* 189.6.

tion has its validity, since individual life has its own irreducible sanctity and every society is composed of individuals doing a variety of different things, not all of which are hostile to its enemies. But an equally valid way of expressing it is that no society may set itself against the existence of another society as such. Acts of just defence and reparation take place at the level of interaction *between* societies, an interaction in which the right of each society to exist must simply be presupposed. Respect is due to the natural forms of social intercourse within any society: its commerce, education, civic communications, distribution of food and so on. Though these functions will undoubtedly suffer "collaterally" in any armed struggle, they are not proper objects of intended destruction.

But the threats on which the deterrent state depends ignore that principle. The question is, does the deterrent state itself ignore it? And do those who form, defend, or acquiesce in deterrence-policy ignore it? In my initial attempt to characterise what is distinctive in modern deterrence-philosophy I drew attention to the great distance that it puts between the intention expressed in a threat and the intention inherent in the act of threatening. From the belief that deterrence can be totally effective if the threat is infinitely enhanced, there arises the conviction that the threatener is not answerable in a straightforward way for intending the acts which he threatens. This is now the point to renew the discussion of intention which I then deferred. Is it true that in intending to keep the peace by threat, the deterrent state does not intend what it threatens? Or does it, by making populations hostage for their governments' good behaviour, turn against the principles of international order and embrace the intention of destroying another society?

Let us begin by setting aside two small terminological points. First, the words "actual intention" are sometimes taken to point to a self-conscious moment of resolve, a moment at which one says "If it be so, so be it!" In that case, it is clear enough that deterrence can get along very well without an "actual intention" to destroy populations. That is not how I use the epithet "actual", and I do not see that such a use would be of interest to the moral thinker. The intention of an act is implied in the structure of the act, and not in some moment of psychological clarity in the actor. Human beings are infinitely capable of concealing from themselves the real implications of their conduct. We do not count a man blameless for the breakdown of his marriage, for example, if he persists in an affair, refusing to acknowledge to himself that one day he will reach the point of walking out on his family. The question about "actual" intention is this: what intentions are *already implied* in the intention to practice deterrence?

Secondly, if an intention is formed subject to a condition, that does not make it any less an actual intention. If somebody resolves, "If she is ever unfaithful, I will kill her", then he has, in effect, formed an actual intention to kill his wife, though only on certain conditions. That is so even if he hopes, and indeed expects, that the conditions will never be realised. Furthermore, if the conditions are very imprecise—"If the worst comes to the worst, I will kill her"—he still intends, actually though remotely, to kill his wife on certain conditions, though he is not clear quite what circumstances will fulfil the conditions. He holds in reserve, as it were, the ready-formed intention. What is sometimes recommended to us as "a mere willingness" to use nuclear weapons seems to amount to something like this: an intention to do so in a remote and ill-defined contingency. It would, of course, be very difficult for a state, or an alliance, to proceed with that degree of unclarity about its policies in practice. Our point here is that it would not resolve the question about intention either, since such willingness would be an actual intention in the morally significant sense.

Mental Reservation and the State

It is clear that an intention to deter implies, in the most direct way, the intention that the threat should be taken seriously by the enemy; which in turn implies the intention that not only certain leaders but the community as a whole should *appear* willing to have the threat executed. This in turn implies that the *official doctrine* of the deterring state must be that in certain circumstances the threat will be made good. An intention to deter, then, implies an intention that the state should maintain this posture formally. So much is hardly open to controversy. The question now arises whether the state can transcend its own formal posture, and whether the individual who urges this posture on the state can transcend it, so that in each case

the intention to commit murder under certain conditions is held, as it were, at arm's length. To transcend
the intention is to make of it a pure instrument, to
which the agent is related like a craftsman to his tool,
deploying it in the service of some quite different intention, which is his real intention, and detaching
himself from it as he does so. Such an exercise, if
possible at all, requires mental reservation—that is,
the capacity in the agent to suspend his own intending while he acts out the "intention" which he has
made the purely instrumental means to effect his own
real intention. Not every intending of instrumental
means, of course, treats the intention-of-the-means itself as a means; and so not every intending of instrumental means requires mental reservation. Of most
intending of means we say, with Kant, "whoever wills
the end wills also the means"[2]—which is to say, the
means as well as the end is part of the project of action
which we have freely chosen and intended. It is only
because the deterrent state is thought to will the end
without quite willing the means, that it becomes necessary to conceive of a "purely instrumental" use of
intention itself as a means, and to stipulate the requirement of mental reservation. But a state is not capable
of practising mental reservation. It is a psychological
possibility only for the individual consciousness.

There are some frequently rehearsed arguments
against the possibility of bluff-deterrence which in fact
carry us further than they are usually made to do,

2. Immanuel Kant, *Fundamental Principles of the Metaphys-
ics of Morals* (Prussian Academy ed. 4.417).

since they amount to disproof of the possibility of mental reservation in a state. We are not ruled by single autocrats. There is no one person, not even the President of the United States, whose private resolutions *ipso facto* constitute a part of the policy of the state. It used to be believed, of course, that this was the case with an absolute monarch. Whether the theory of absolute monarchy ever really did justice to the political realities it attempted to describe may be doubted; but the point is of no practical importance. In a modern state a policy must be able to be found, somewhere or other, in the files. But even that is not enough. Imagine a small group of senior ministers, including the Head of Government, and armed-forces chiefs meeting in secret conclave and making a solemn agreement never to press the button; and grant them one locked filing-cabinet to keep their plans in. What you have there is not a policy of the state but a conspiracy. The conspiracy may be overthrown in course of time by changes of personnel, and the filing-cabinet may sit there unopened and forgotten. Or the emergency may arise and the conspirators' plans may go into effect, attempting to stop in its tracks the enormous programmed machinery of national and international crisis-management in circumstances of great public panic. Even should those plans succeed, it would mean simply that the policy of the state had been overthrown by a conspiracy. Such private plans could not themselves be state policy. (They must be distinguished, of course, from the exercise of discretion that might be allowed to such a group *within* the policy of the state, to determine the when and the where of its implementation.) We know, of course, that there can be official secrets; but the broad lines of defence policy cannot be a secret, for too many thousands of people, military and civilian, are involved in planning it and carrying it through. On the question of whether the deterrent could ever be used, the policy of the state must be what the policy of the state is generally known to be, and it cannot be something else. The state has no way of transcending its posture of willingness to use disproportionate and indiscriminate force. Its intention is its policy and its policy its intention. So the intention to deter implies, at least, an intention that the *state* should intend to carry out its threats.

The Individual Transcending the State

But perhaps that is not fatal. After all, it might be argued, if the state is incapable of mental reservation, by the very same token its intentions are not susceptible of moral evaluation on the same terms as those of individuals. If the intentions of the state are nothing more than the policies proclaimed in its name, then they are not intentions in the morally assessable sense. Cannot the individual, precisely because he does have the power of mental reservation, transcend the policies of the state and use them as an instrumental means for the good purposes of deterring war, while at the same time detaching himself from the bad purposes they express of conducting unrestrained war? Here, I believe, we reach the core of this argument for arm's-length intention, and it becomes apparent that it is an intensely individualistic one. It rests on an exaggerated idealist conception of the individual's capacity to detach himself from the political will of the community.

The agent, on this account, is someone whose intention that the state should intend the destruction of populations does not imply a corresponding intention of his own. He simply transcends the state as a craftsman transcends his tool, rather than engaging in it as a participant in its political life. This is quite unreal. In the case of some state *other* than that which gives form to the political life of my own community, I could perhaps will that it should have a certain policy without making that policy my own. A Briton, for example, might wish that isolationism may not prevail in American political life, since it carries with it such uncomfortable consequences for Europe; and yet he might think that, were he an American, he would be a moderate isolationist. An American might wish the British would be more accommodating to Argentina over the Falkland Islands because tension over the question destabilises the South American continent; yet were he a Briton, he might think, he would not wish to be very accommodating. But with one's own state one cannot will the state to do things without willing the things one wills the state to do. The state is a corporate agent which derives its agency from that of its participating members. I am a political agent, though a minor one. Even if I am not enfranchised, I am a small part of that wider public whose consent determines the limits within which the state is free to act. My views on what the state should do are those of a participant in political deliberation; I am therefore responsible for their implications. I cannot consistently demand the return of hanging and then be angry when someone is hanged. Similarly I cannot require the state to be willing to wage counter-population war in certain emergencies and then express dismay if, when those emergencies arise, it does so. Not, that is, without acknowledging some responsibility for the miscalculation.

The unreality is thrown into sharper relief when the claim is reinforced with the argument that the deterrer can *know* that deterrence will be successful, and therefore does not have to contemplate or frame an intention for the situation in which deterrence breaks down. This merely renders obvious the abstract character of this agent who is supposed to intend deterrence without intending the acts of war which deterrence threatens. He is someone who knows, as a matter of moral certainty, that which no earthly being can possibly know about the consequences of his willing. The mere fact that he *wills* the acts that he threatens provides the ground of his *knowledge* that those acts will never be required; and this knowledge is then invoked to fence off the purely hypothetical character of his will and so deliver him from responsibility for it. Notoriously, it is the description of just one agent in the universe that his will constitutes the immediate ground of his foreknowledge, and that is God. The connexion between will and foreknowledge in divine action has here been parodically inverted: whereas God, in willing, knows that what he wills will be, the agent of deterrence knows that what he wills will not be. The difference made by the inversion is surprisingly small. It is the immediacy of the connexion which marks the deterrent agent off from all other human agents and identifies him as a variety of the fantastic creator-man of technology, who posits by his will-to-create the very world that he foreknows. But the creator-man is fantastic, not real. The claims of deterrence to direct world-history by the immediate power of the will are without substantial ground. They have lost their foundation in the real goods of social and political existence.

Renouncing Penultimate Measures

Once we have reached this conclusion, we may be tempted to think that we have seen right through the deterrent and may join cheerfully in the laughter of him that dwelleth in heaven. If the posture of deterrence has cut itself off from the realities of social existence, then it is simply ridiculous. The emperor who has no clothes has no dignity or authority either. What we may forget, however, is that every quest for an insubstantial good proceeds by the rejection of real goods. We learn from the Apocalypse again that the empty charade of the divinised state can achieve a frightening solidity before the blast of reality scatters it to the winds. We underestimate deterrence, then, if we merely acknowledge that it is impotent to do good. Because it implies the intention in the last resort to destroy populations, it embraces at an ultimate level the will to do evil, to attack the order of international peace. At the penultimate level, moreover, it is equally hostile to the order of international peace, since it involves a refusal to do good.

We recall that all deterrence tends to become mutual deterrence. The implication of this is that it involves a renunciation of a peculiar sort. The deterrent state renounces the right to take decisive *penultimate* military action, or steps leading to it, to remedy *moderately serious* international injustices, whenever such action might be felt by its opponent to be hostile. Consider the cases of Hungary, Czechoslovakia, and Poland, three nations which, in the course of the deterrence-age, have risen in armed revolt or major political agitation in an attempt to loosen the shackles of an alien empire and establish an order not only of greater independence but of greater justice. The moral sympathies of the West were deeply engaged in each case, but the West could do nothing to help. It is possible that even in conventional circumstances the West would have had only limited responses open to it. Not even the freedom of these nations, we might have thought, could justify the risk of another major European war. But that question never came to be decided on its merits, because a prior decision had ruled it out of order. That decision, implicit in the logic of deterrence, was to freeze the existing limits of the Soviet sphere of influence. The character of the peace which deterrence ensured was an indefinite prolongation of the status quo along the border between the two blocs.

At this point deterrence most resembles pacifism. In order to preserve the balance, we renounce the right to intervene in a just cause with military force.

The objection made in the name of diplomatic wisdom against pacifism applies with equal force against deterrence: it cannot be right to renounce in advance the option of using arms to confront proportionally grave injustice. Force, crude as it is, is at the service of justice and order, and it may sometimes be necessary at least to contemplate it. To refuse to contemplate it is to render the negotiated pursuit of a just international order impotent. Of the arts and methods of international politics as we have traditionally conceived them Geoffrey Goodwin has written finely:

> One of the diplomatic arts is to discern the changing configurations of power amongst the more powerful and to work for their more orderly management, whether jointly or collectively, whilst at the same time responding to the interests of the less powerful and to the need to remedy the more glaring injustices in international society, the persistence of which may threaten the very international order it is desired to uphold.[3]

The tendency of deterrence is to render the practice of these humane and realistic arts impossible, since it forbids the configurations of power to change and inhibits attention to the interests of the less powerful. To the instance of Eastern Europe we may add one other example which may strike British citizens with special force, instructed as they have been by the reminiscences marking the fifth anniversary of their brief war in the South Atlantic. It was the doctrinal preoccupa-

3. In *Ethics and Nuclear Deterrence,* ed. Geoffrey Goodwin (Croom Helm, 1982), p. 19.

tion of Mr. John Nott, the Defence Secretary, with the sufficiency of nuclear deterrence that left the British navy all but disarmed against the Argentine invasion of the Falkland Islands.

It would be absurd to deny, of course, that diplomatic arts have continued to be practised in the deterrence-age. Indeed, wars have been fought, though only at some distance from the delicate European border which divides the blocs. Whatever doctrines prevail, international politics is necessary to the world, and the world will pursue it. States will seek more room to manoeuvre, they will form new alliances in place of old, and the morally self-confident communities will lift their voices against the others to demand such reforms as human rights and democratic liberty. This is, no doubt, as it should be, and deterrence will not prevent it. But the goals of deterrence and the goals of traditional politics are at war with each other. The continuing vitality of international politics, with its wide range of interests beyond that of deterring attack, is one of the factors that deny deterrence the power to fulfil its promise of a stable peace and drive it into the cyclical oscillations on which we commented in the last chapter. The superior realism of the traditional politics allows us to be certain that deterrence will not, in fact, lay down the rules for a future world. In that it aims to render the present international blocs permanent as the price for avoiding war between them, it is obvious that its aim is unrealisable. Empires crumble because those who belong to them, and sometimes those outside them, become disenchanted with their position. They complain of unjust treatment, and the power-centres of the empire find themselves too weak to resist the pressure put upon them. It may be regarded as morally certain that the erosion of discontent will eventually lay low the two empires that now confront each other over the Berlin wall. Things will not remain as they are for ever, because politics is an expression of human vitality and is not susceptible to the deep-freezing treatment which deterrence has tried to practise upon it.

But we must ask, then, what deterrence actually *has* contributed to the international situation of our time, since we disallow, on the one hand, the claim that it has made no difference at all, and refuse to credit it, on the other, with all the elements of stability which derive in fact from the more traditional conduct of international politics which has continued alongside it. What it has done is to introduce such an element of rigidity into the boundary between the two empires that the idea of any shift in the boundary becomes increasingly alarming. The empires must crumble some day, yet it is almost inconceivable that they can do so without nuclear war. The strategy for avoiding nuclear war, therefore, becomes that of shoring up increasingly unstable empires and alliances—a strategy which is unattractive to anyone with an ounce of genuine political realism in his make-up. To this we must add that the rigidity of direct East-West confrontation in the past four decades has only been managed by the maintenance of a good deal of flexibility elsewhere: the battles between the blocs have been fought in Vietnam, Afghanistan, and Nicaragua. Now imagine what must follow if the existing rigidity of the European front is expanded elsewhere by the proliferation of nuclear capabilities to other states, some of them already perpetrating appalling injustices. At this point the very thought of an ordered pursuit of international justice seems to vanish over the horizon, leaving us with the prospect of a world-map dissected into untouchable spheres of influence. But since we have every reason to think that human communities cannot live in such a world, we have to conclude simply that the achievement of deterrence has been to make international politics exceedingly dangerous.

It is worth pausing here to clarify the status of this reference to danger within the structure of the argument, lest anyone should think that, after all, the whole debate comes down to rival assertions of good or harmful consequences. The attribution of consequences to deterrence is itself necessarily theory-dependent. There is no "objective" way of observing what follows from deterrence—that is to say, there is no way that does not begin from an interpretation of what deterrence is and an analysis of its primary aims. Those who attribute to this source such elements of stability as the present international order possesses do so not by right of an independently observable connexion but because the theory of deterrence they advance requires them to. Similarly, my own account of the harm done by deterrence to international politics arises from what I have said about the posture of the deterrent will itself. There is no great difficulty about this. Those who have not been taken in by the textbooks of ethics that divide everybody into "deontologists" and "teleologists" understand perfectly well that a wrongful act is liable to produce harm and that the wrongfulness of an act can sometimes be inferred from the harm it does. In pointing to the new difficulties faced by international politics in our age, I simply complete the account I have given of the wrongfulness of the deterrent will and substantiate the observation that it includes the refusal to pursue appropriate political goods in appropriate political ways.

Our account, then, is this: that there are two complementary orientations of the deterrent will, one of them *refusing* the use of proportionate and moderate force to realise limited aims of international justice, the other *embracing* the destruction of whole populations in extreme circumstances. The sin of commission (which has been embraced by the will though not yet acted upon, rather like when someone reserves the possibility of killing himself, though hoping it will never come to that) corresponds exactly to the sin of omission. In exposition it looks as though the sin of omission arises out of the sin of commission. At the deepest level of motivation, however, the order is the opposite. The sin of omission has necessitated the sin of commission. Our simple refusal to risk moderate and limited conflict for the international good has led us to be willing to do the immoderate and the unlimited. At the heart of deterrence is war-weariness. But war-weariness is not the same as love of peace. A positive love of peace leads one to search for the conditions of just peace and to strive to maintain them by such exertions as are appropriate. War-weariness refuses to make the exertion, and looks for labour-saving ways of keeping the peace.

Erosion of Liberal Values

Consequences may be either proximate or remote; and at this point we turn to the remote consequences, those which were not implicit in the orientation of the will from the beginning, but which have come upon us unforeseen and unlooked-for as a result of the failure of deterrence to do what we expected of it. We have spoken of the things which we have willed that we ought not to have willed, and of the things which we have not willed that we ought to have willed, and now we must confess that God's just judgment has fallen upon us.

That judgment is the erosion and disappearance of the liberal political values which the West thought it was defending. This follows not from the project of deterrence itself, which was to avoid war, but from the inevitable failure of deterrence, which has left us once again contemplating the possibility of war, but of war now potentially inflated in the magnitude of its devastating potential to the point where it is disproportionate to any humane political goal. The choice that confronts us once we recognise that war has not in fact been made impossible is a simple one: either to acknowledge the failure as failure, and restructure our defences towards the conduct of truly limited war, one which would be proportionate in scale to humane political goals; or to revise completely our traditional conceptions of what will count as reasonable political goals. If we take, as we have done so far, the second course, we enter on a new phase in the collapse of deterrence. We begin to justify the kind of war which was

intended to be constitutionally insusceptible of justi-
fication. In so doing we lose touch with the liberal
political values that have nourished Western civilisation. Liberal values, of course, are not the only form in
which the social and political good can offer itself to
our understanding, and there is much scope for criticism of Western liberalism. Nevertheless, it represents
a certain form of political good, and, in particular, the
form which we inherited. It is no minor disaster to lose
our hold upon it.

If we take ultimate disproportion into the category
of eligible means, we can do so only at the cost of re-
vising our conceptions of the eligible end. The justifi-
cation of nuclear war creates its own scale of values. It
regards the destruction of Western civilisation, with its
unforeseeable attendant suffering possibly lasting for
centuries, as preferable to the subjection of Western
civilisation to alien political conditions. Whatever may
be said in favour of such a judgment, it can claim no
continuity with the liberal tradition of thought. It has
invested a political order with sanctions appropriate
to an ultimate value; and "liberalism", if it meant anything, meant a political vision which treated all political orders as *relative* values. In the liberal tradition
political order had to be justified in terms of some
greater good, which was understood as the freedom
of individuals to achieve their legitimate aspirations.
There was no sacred order, merely some orders that
were preferable to others in that they facilitated individual self-fulfilment more successfully. Within the
liberal tradition the central commitment was to the
continued possibility of such fulfilment, so that the

choice of political forms in each social situation was ordered pragmatically to that end. That is why liberal traditions have in the past proved adaptable and capable of accommodating a wide variety of social needs. The laissez-faire economic policies of the so-called neo-conservatives and the human rights activism of the centrist left can each claim to be an interpretation of liberal values. But when someone thinks that it would be better for there to be *no* conditions for individual fulfilment than for the present satisfactory ones to be replaced with others less satisfactory, then he has categorically left the liberal tradition behind him, embracing a form of political totalitarianism.

Some political goods cannot be defended by some political means, and among the pairs of incompatibles are traditional liberalism and civilisation-destroying acts of war. So that when someone suggests that circumstances might *in extremis* necessitate resort to all-out nuclear war, we know that he cannot be proposing to defend liberal values against their assailants. In his mind the inherited liberalism of the West has been supplanted by a new political commitment which matches totalitarian claim with totalitarian claim. It may be that this shift from liberal to neo-liberal values is already discernible in the social changes which have been so marked a feature of the post-war Western world. We have come to demand ideological purity in place of tolerant flexibility. We have striven to maximize equality of access to life-enhancing material resources while narrowing the field of claimants, excluding children *in utero,* defective newborns, and whole populations of developing nations. The pragmatism of traditional liberalism has given way to a revolutionary passion, marked by anxious intolerance of differences, populist egalitarianism, and an internationalist suspicion of local boundaries. Even the code-word "democracy", which sums up our commitment most succinctly, has come to mean something different in terms of actual political structures—not least in North America, where the powers of elected legislatures have been systematically eroded by the expanding jurisdiction of appointed courts. There is a great deal more to be said about these changes than I can pretend to say, and these remarks are only intended to point to a line of speculation which may possibly prove fruitful. But is it not, at least, worthy of observation that in the very era when we have claimed to defend Western liberalism by resort to ultimate sanction, the content of that liberalism has undergone unprecedented change and become subject to far-reaching uncertainty?

We can focus the observation best, perhaps, with the help of a myth. When Adam and Eve left the Garden of Eden, they said to one another: "It is not right that we who have dwelt in Paradise should wander over the face of the earth, struggling to maintain civilisation against plague, famine, drought and storm, wild beasts and every kind of hardship. Let us make ourselves a new Garden of Eden as good as the old." So they marked out a well-favoured site just across from the place they had left, and subdued it; yet the wild beasts continued to knock down its hedges and the storms continued to flatten its crops. Then Adam said to Eve: "Let us borrow fire from heaven, and set it at the gate of our garden to frighten the beasts and keep the storms away." So he crept by night to where the angel stood with the flaming sword, guarding the way to the tree of life, and lighting a brand from the fire of that sword carried it back to the gate of his own garden. There he built a pyre with a flame that rose to heaven, answering the flame of the angel's sword on the other side of the valley. Behind this pyre Adam and Eve made their home in comfort and safety. On the first day the fire began to spread around the perimeter of the garden, and wherever they had dug, planted or trimmed, the fire protected it, but wherever there was wilderness the fire burned, and soon they were enclosed within a wall of fire, and they lived there free of wild beasts, storms, plague and famine, bringing their garden to order. Then one day a small corner on the perimeter, where Adam had forgotten to prune the fruit trees and cut back the briars, was engulfed in fire. The next day a patch of vegetables overgrown with weeds was burning; and on the third day an old sheep, heavy with unshorn wool, was lost in the flames. Soon the relentless law became apparent: wherever there was disorder in the garden the flame encroached, and inch by inch the garden was reduced in size. More than ever Adam and Eve tilled the ground and kept the trees and cared for the animals. The once carefree charm of their garden became a model of order and system, while that which had been a pleasure and triumph to them became a fearful burden. Yet hard as they worked, from morning to night and on into the long hours of darkness, rising again before dawn to take up their task, somewhere each day the flame found fault. They tried to simplify their labours: they slaughtered the animals that roamed wild, and put the rest in pens; they dug out the bushes that straggled and planted in straight rows; but all to no avail, for relentlessly the flames moved in.

The myth is as yet unfinished. What is to become of the Promethean race which thought it could use heavenly fire to protect itself?

CHAPTER V

Peacemaking

A NY ATTEMPT to have done with deterrence must imply a programme of disarmament. I say "imply" because the two ideas are not identical: deterrence is not a kind of armament, and being rid of it is not a matter of changing military equipment but of changing how we think. In principle, therefore, we could abandon deterrence in as long as it takes to change our minds, without a single measure of actual disarmament. But then the question would arise of how we were to arm ourselves appropriately to the proper purposes of international politics: to use measured force, and only measured force, as might be necessary in extreme circumstances to maintain the order and justice of nations. Our present nuclear forces are unfitted for such purposes; some of them are intrinsically disproportionate to any conceivable military goal, others probably disproportionate to any likely military goal, the whole greatly in excess of any rational political function. An emancipation of our thinking from the dogmas of deterrence, then, would be bound to leave us contemplating a measure of nuclear disarmament. We would be irresponsible to forget that it would also suggest the strengthening of military preparedness in other ways.

The topic of disarmament has so dominated discussion of deterrence that in popular debate contributors are classified entirely by their answer to the one question, "Is disarmament to be achieved unilaterally or multilaterally?" This has the ironic result, as Anthony Kenny observes, that "those who wish to preserve a massive nuclear arsenal describe themselves as 'multilateral disarmers', and an increase in the nuclear armoury . . . is described as a step towards a real reduction in nuclear arms."[1] It might seem, then, that nothing need be said about this topic in general debate. For if we were really agreed that disarmament must happen, it could safely be left to the strategists to work out how. But since the question continues to prove vexatiously contentious, we ought to conclude that we have never been agreed on whether to disarm in the first place, nor even on the more fundamental matter, what our armaments are meant to achieve. That is to say, the mode of disarmament is the wrong question to focus on, since it begs other very important questions and is not an important question itself.

Nevertheless, it demands a little of our attention, and that precisely because it *is* the wrong question. If matters of principle and matters of practical im-

1. Anthony Kenny, *The Logic of Deterrence* (Firethorn, 1985), p. ix. Reasons for this, arising from the confusion of arms control and arms reduction, are suggested by George Weigel, *Tranquillitas Ordinis* (Oxford University Press, 1987), pp. 360ff.

plementation could be sharply distinguished in the public mind, it would be possible to leave the latter to those who were charged with exercising prudence on our behalf. But because questions of principle keep raising themselves afresh under the guise of purely prudential deliberations, the moral thinker must remain on guard, not in order to instruct the experts on what is practicable (which is not within his competence) but in order to remind them as often as may be necessary of what is unprincipled. We may take a pastoral analogy. It is, in general terms, a bad confessor who thinks he can instruct a penitent in detail on the steps of reparation and amendment which ought to accompany conversion. Once the penitent has repented, there is place for the grace of God and particular prudential judgment in mapping out the way of amendment. A married man who supports a mistress repents of his adultery: what is he to do with his mistress? The confessor's advice should be very circumspect, apart from insisting that he should not continue in his adultery. But if the penitent adulterer declares that he will keep his mistress indefinitely in his household, is this not a sign that, after all, he is ambivalent about his repentance? The conscientious pastor could hardly fail to warn him of the possibility. And if the deterrent states have now signed a treaty to abolish land-based intermediate-range weapons (of lesser destructiveness) and expressed the hope of signing another to reduce, but not abolish, intercontinental and submarine-based strategic weapons (of greater destructiveness), can the conscientious pastor fail to observe, in between the glasses of champagne and the congratulatory speeches about sleeping easier in our beds, that this bespeaks an unshaken confidence in deterrence—a return, indeed, to the more brazen form of the belief, in which "massive" rather than "flexible" response is to be the key to our security?

But then, nobody ever claimed that the *deterrent states* had repented their sins of thought, word and deed. Altogether more surprising is the ambiguity which affects *opponents* of deterrence precisely when they consider how we may proceed to disarm. Amendment, of course, may be a slow and confused business; and no one has a right to complain if a programme for abandoning deterrence does not accomplish everything at a stroke. The most determined traveller has still to get from here to there by some practicable route. The point is that in devising a route one should make no theoretical concessions which undermine the point of the journey. "We must go to Guernsey to buy our cream; so let's go through Devon because there are good cows there, too!" At the heart of an effective critique of deterrence lies the discovery that it cannot give what it promises, that it is an idol unworthy of our worship and confidence. It offers a perverse view of reality. A programme for rejecting deterrence, then, should not be argued on the basis of some contention which those who reject deterrence are supposed not to believe. Other programmes for "arms control" may do as they please. "Deterrence" and "nuclear weapons" are not synonymous; neither is rejecting deterrence identical with nuclear disarmament.

Yet it can seem as though the doctrines of deterrence return to us time and time again from the mouths of professed sceptics. In a much-quoted saying Pope John Paul II conceded that "in current conditions deterrence based on balance, certainly not as an end in itself but as a step on the way towards progressive disarmament, may still be judged morally acceptable."[2] Where did he get the idea that the "balance" offered by deterrence could be a "step" on the way to anything? Barrie Paskins, that most elegant advocate of unilateral disarmament, counsels unilateralists to argue "that deterrence is robust rather than delicate."[3] What is this robustness that we are to attribute to it other than a capacity to give peace? Anthony Kenny, in arguing that submarine-launched strategic missiles should be the last to be abandoned in a programme of disarmament, admits it as a paradox of nuclear weapons that "those which are most objectionable in terms of their murderous potential are often those which are least dangerous from the point of view of political strategy."[4] How does this "paradox" differ from the "contradictions" of deterrence which he rightly criticises? The Archbishop of Canterbury has recommended an "attempt to ban and scrap battlefield weapons which contribute to the illusion that limited and tactical nuclear war is pos-

2. Message to the U.N. Special Session on Disarmament, June 1982. Quoted in David Hollenbach, *Nuclear Ethics* (Paulist Press, 1983), p. 76.

3. Barrie Paskins, "Deep Cuts are Morally Imperative", in *Ethics and Nuclear Deterrence,* ed. Geoffrey Goodwin (Croom Helm, 1982), p. 103.

4. Kenny, *Logic of Deterrence,* p. 100.

sible."[5] And the Catholic Bishops of the United States, arguing in the same cause, advocate "removal . . . of short-range nuclear weapons which multiply dangers disproportionate to their deterrent value."[6] From whom did these church leaders learn that the closer a weapon comes to realistic war-fighting scale, the more unstable is the relation between the states which possess it? If the consistency of these remarks is to be defended, it can only be by becoming clearer about a question of principle which emerges from each of them: how much can be claimed for the existing deterrence strategy as a *provisional* measure of stability if its claims to provide a *permanent* stability are rejected? Can we consistently say that deterrence does not fulfil its promises, and still argue that in departing from it we have to protect the balance it has achieved?

5. Speech at British Council of Churches debate, November 1980. Quoted in Goodwin, ed., *Ethics and Nuclear Deterrence*, p. 192.

6. *The Challenge of Peace: God's Promise and Our Response*, A Pastoral Letter on War and Peace of the National Conference of Catholic Bishops (U.S. Catholic Conference, 1983), p. 60. I am aware that neither the Archbishop of Canterbury nor the U.S. Catholic bishops have formally committed themselves to opposing deterrence. They have, however, permitted themselves such abhorrence of the *status quo* that they must be counted among those who *reject* the claim that deterrence assures a stable peace. Abhorrence, like all intellectual luxuries, must be paid for; and the price, in this case, is maintaining positions that are consistent with this rejection.

Alleged Dangers of Disarmament

We must start from the common point of departure: the deterrent cannot deliver what it promises. We should, perhaps, make up our minds first of all that nothing good would be lost if the West were simply without it. It gives us no permanent stability, and therefore no security and no release of international tension. Such stability as currently obtains in the international situation derives from other sources, such as non-deterrent defences, the common interests of the major parties and the special interests that each side has in avoiding (conventional) war. These stabilising elements would still be present if the NATO alliance lacked the deterrent. This is the perception that properly undergirds the case for a unilateral initiative. The investor who decides that his shares will never yield a profit gets rid of them without waiting to see what others will do. If he delays, we may presume that he still hopes they may redeem themselves. But the deterrent will not redeem itself. If our opponents follow our unilateral example, we may think, well and good. If they do not, the loss is all theirs, for they will find themselves servicing an expensive white elephant. This, as I say, is the true form of the case for a unilateral initiative, and it rests on two premises: first, that each side in a conflict is inevitably the unilateral judge of its own interests; secondly, that neither side could find it in its own interests to possess a nuclear deterrent. Multilateral initiatives are only necessary or possible when each side judges (unilaterally) that it is in its own interest to balance its movements very carefully to those of the other; but that can arise only when there are *real* interests on either side that could be won or lost by imbalance. But to understand what is wrong with deterrence is to understand that there are no such interests.

This argument, it seems to me, cannot be faulted until the last step. But there it ignores the real interest that each side has in avoiding danger; for there are, indeed, dangers in disarmament. But it is useful as a thought-experiment, since it brings to light the ambiguity which surrounds all talk about the dangers of disarmament, namely, that it may simply be a way of praising deterrence in other words. The dangers of disarmament do not arise from the mere circumstance of having no deterrent while the other side has one. For if the deterrent does no good, then our lack of it would deprive us of no good. We must distinguish between the *alleged* dangers of unilaterally *not having* a deterrent and the *real* dangers of unilaterally *laying aside* a deterrent which we now have.

Let us elaborate the one side of this distinction in relation to the so-called "nuclear blackmail" to which, it is often supposed, any disarmed party would be open. Those who speak of that danger rarely permit us to see what kind of scenario they have in mind, and I must confess that I have been unable to imagine a plausible one myself. But we may briefly review some possibilities. In the first place, suppose that our enemy is hell-bent on conquest and domination. For an enemy with these ambitions to threaten the use of high-yield nuclear missiles against territories which it intended to occupy would be quite incredible. Badly contaminated territories are not conquerable. Suppose, then, the opposite extreme, that the enemy is not bent on conquest, but is responding to what it perceives as a threat to its own vital interests from conventional or tactical nuclear attack. In such a situation there would certainly be the risk of a strategic nuclear strike; but this risk would be present irrespective of whether we had a deterrent. For the rules of the deterrence-age are those of non-interference, and even under the conditions that now obtain the appearance of a threat to an enemy's vital interest risks nuclear war. All that would be lost by unilateral disarmament would be the capacity to retaliate—to no political purpose, but merely for vengeance's sake. Suppose, thirdly, a scenario somewhere between these two extremes: an enemy on an expansive political course, aiming to extend its sphere of influence but not to overwhelm the other power-bloc, might threaten strategic nuclear attack in order to neutralise opposition to diplomatic or military gains elsewhere. Here, I would think, is the most plausible programme for "nuclear blackmail"; but this, too, could happen equally well where deterrence was mutual. (As things stand now, we might ask, for what purposes would the United States be prepared to enter a nuclear war? To defend Iran? To defend West Berlin?) Furthermore, the diplomatic losses of such a move in terms of influence and goodwill among uncommitted nations would be likely to outweigh the immediate gains, so that there would still be strong political considerations to deter it, even if there were no "deterrent".

We ought to consider, too, that any nuclear power

which was open to reprisal attack from conventional forces, possibly reinforced by battlefield nuclear weapons, could be deterred from strategic attack simply by the knowledge that it could not use contaminating weapons *against an invading army*. The great disincentive to a Soviet strike against European or American cities is a strong military capability situated along the Iron Curtain. Western strategic disarmament would simply throw the weight of European defence back where it belonged, on its capacity to conduct damaging reprisal invasions of Eastern Europe and the U.S.S.R.[7] None of this, of course, makes it *impossible* that Western Europe or America (or indeed the U.S.S.R.) would ever be the victim of strategic nuclear attack if it were to renounce the deterrent unilaterally. It merely indicates that danger will arise, not from the lack of a deterrent to frighten such attack off, but from a combination of risk-taking and international panic which would be highly dangerous in any circumstances, with or without bilateral deterrence. The likelihood of such a situation arising would be no greater, and quite possibly less, if unilateral strategic disarmament had taken place.

We may add in passing a comment on the Cuban

7. The greatest danger of NATO's current military dispositions is undoubtedly its paucity of troops, which are hardly such as to allow effective pursuit of an invading Warsaw Pact army, even should it prove possible to hold an invasion at bay. To be able to frustrate an invasion without being able to repel it is an invitation to the enemy to escalate to the nuclear level, since it promises that all the collateral damage of war will be absorbed on the Western, not the Eastern, side of the Iron Curtain.

missile crisis of 1962, often taken as the canonical example of the power of the nuclear deterrent to deter. Depending on how you view the events which led up to it, you will judge that the occasion for the crisis lay either in Soviet expansionism or in an American threat to vital Soviet interests. The diplomatic basis on which the problem was solved was a concession by the United States that Cuba lay within the Soviet sphere of influence. If, then, the Soviet presence in Cuba was a case of Soviet expansionism, it succeeded. If the American attempt to unseat Castro was a threat to vital Soviet interests, it failed. Politically the American deterrent achieved nothing for its possessor. Militarily, it secured the removal of Soviet missile bases from Cuba, an insubstantial triumph which restored the status quo, since the missile bases would hardly have been placed there if there had been no American threat to Cuba in the first place. This degree of military security was purchased by the concession of America's original political goals with respect to Cuba. The deterrent did nothing except to bring the world within inches of nuclear war.

Real Dangers of Disarmament

Let us concede, then, this element of the unilateral case. We cannot lose by being rid of a deterrent which does nothing to protect us. Yet now we must concede something in the other direction. The *process* of unilateral disarmament may be perilous, and safety requires that we achieve an element of multilateral understanding. To say this is not to admit that deterrence "works". It does not presuppose any real stability in the stable balance of terror. It merely supposes that the reigning doctrine, believed at official level by enemy and ally alike, declares that there is such a stability and that any change in posture will be destabilizing because it will cause alarm to the other side. We can consistently allow this one valid, if ironic, sense to the notion of "deterrent stability": in that deterrence provides a form of mutual understanding, it is more stable than a situation in which either side is afraid that it cannot read the other's intentions and acts in panic.[8]

Unilateral initiative, then, must be well-prepared-for if it is not to present the danger of being unintel-

8. There is, I think, a second sense of this phrase which we can consistently admit: that deterrence stability consists in "the inability of either (side) to mount a crippling first strike against the other" (Weigel, *Tranquillitas Ordinis*, p. 302). That is to say, instability would consist in the incapacity of either side to mount an effective retaliation. But an effective retaliation does not have to be a retaliation *in kind,* a point that has long been recognised by apologists for the independent British and French nuclear deterrents. Our point is that *conventional retaliation* can be effective, so that nuclear disarmament will be destabilising in this sense only if it is carried through without an appropriate strengthening of conventional forces. (See Lawrence Freedman, "The Conventional Option", in *What Hope in an Armed World?*, ed. Richard Harries [Pickering & Inglis, 1982], pp. 28-48.) Thus Weigel's conviction that somewhere in the course of genuine disarmament strategic defensive systems will be required does not seem to be necessary, though his recommendation that this should be in a "mutual or common security framework" avoids the difficulties of strategic defence *within* deterrence which we outlined on pp. 62f.

ligible to a highly suspicious adversary. The first task in disarmament is to replace the current artificial forms of mutual understanding, by which we hope to make ourselves predictable to our enemies, with more serviceable ones. It is easy to see how well-intentioned unilateral measures to establish a limited and proportionate defence capability in the West might appear threatening to an adversary who did not appreciate their motivation—especially if there were a sudden transfer of resources away from strategic arms to the conventional military presence in Europe. It is the priority of communication which makes it important to sustain the bilateral approach to disarmament for as long as it continues to carry us forward. Yet there are two quite different doctrines that make a "multilateralist"—leaving aside the kind of multilaterist who does not seriously intend disarmament at all. One is that what needs to be done can *only* be done bilaterally; the other is that what needs to be done is *better* done bilaterally but *must* be done somehow. The latter doctrine makes the kind of multilateralist who is prepared to be a unilateralist if negotiated disarmament stops, driven not by a self-sacrificial morality fit only for heroes and saints but by a clear understanding of the political good which it is the task of political prudence to pursue. Only the latter kind of multilateralist (who is also, at the same time, a kind of unilateralist) can be thought to have grasped the point of disarmament, which is to get out of a posture which is ineffective politically and impossible to sustain.

Such a multilateralist would, I suppose, be driven to contemplate at least this much of a unilateral initiative should bilateral approaches to disarmament come to a halt: most importantly, a unilateral undertaking that existing strategic forces will not be replaced by new ones of comparable or greater capability (thus avoiding the shock of sudden withdrawals); a slow, well-prepared build-up of usable battle-fighting forces, either at conventional or at the lowest nuclear level, subject to a renewed invitation to negotiate common limits on this level; these to be accompanied by a sustained attempt to communicate a philosophy of purely proportionate defence and by confidence-creating moves to alleviate any existing perceived threats to the enemy's security. It is not guaranteed safe, but it offers such safety as could reasonably be hoped for in the circumstances, and considerably more than would be offered by the perpetuation of deterrence. So much, perhaps, is sufficient (and more than this would be obtrusive) for a theologian to say about the mode in which disarmament should be pursued.

The Goal of Disarmament

But the mode is not the only aspect of disarmament which invites his questioning. It is more important, and more germane to the theologian's primary concerns, to ask questions about the goal. If deterrence is at fault partly because of its ill-conceived utopian goal, it is doubly important that a programme of disarmament, undertaken to correct the mistakes of modern deterrence, should be entirely realistic about what it hopes to achieve. It is from every point of view a difficult task to rid ourselves of those hopes of "perpetual peace" which have generated and sustained the policies of deterrence. Does it follow, then, that we have nothing but a sequence of "just wars" to look forward to? And if we say so, can we really defend, from the point of view of Christian theology, a hard-nosed realism that will embrace this as the best that can be hoped for, and reject deterrence, as it were, with the complaint that it makes just wars too difficult to fight? It seems that we may have to pay for our possession of the low ground of realism by surrendering the high ground of Christian peacemaking; that may be a theological price that is simply prohibitive.

The resolution of this difficulty lies by way of a clearer articulation of the multivalent notion of peace. Peace is a great variety of conditions. "The peace of the body," says Augustine,

> is the temperate ordering of its parts, the peace of the rational soul the orderly congruence of knowledge and action; the peace of the body and the soul is the ordered and secure life of the animate being; the peace of mortal men and God is the ordered obedience of faith to the eternal law; the peace of man is harmonious agreement; the peace of the household an ordered agreement among those who dwell together about commanding and obeying; the peace of the city is an agreement among citizens about commanding and obeying; the peace of the heavenly city is a society of utmost order and agreement in the enjoyment of God and of one another in God; the peace of the universe is the tranquillity of order.[9]

9. Augustine, *De civitate Dei* XIX.13.1.

In the face of this we need to pray for the grace of discrimination. I propose to order my remarks around a prayer which perfectly responds to the need. It asks: "Show us, good Lord, the peace we should seek, the peace we must give, the peace we can keep, the peace we must forgo, and the peace you have given in Jesus our Lord."[10]

The prayer starts from the indeterminate peace which forms the horizon of our hopes, and asks that we may be shown where that horizon is properly located: "Show us, good Lord, the peace we should seek." It then moves back to the middle-ground of human action and renunciation: "the peace we must give, the peace we can keep, the peace we must forgo", and finally out to the horizon again: "the peace you have given in Jesus our Lord." But on reaching the horizon for the second time, it has discerned its true determination. That final peace is no longer simply the ill-defined object of all our aspirations, the empty space in the future to which our hopes reach out in blind grasping. It is now the formed gift of God, the rule of Jesus Christ, already present to us through faith, for which we look in hope as the full disclosure of what we already know and possess. Christian striving for peace arises within this eschatological horizon, on the basis of God's gift once given, in the hope of a promise that is not vague but precisely determined. The presence of Jesus as Lord is the reality which we know and the shape of the future for which we hope. The

10. *The Oxford Book of Prayer* (Oxford University Press, 1985), p. 80.

point at issue between political "idealism" and political "realism" is not, as was influentially claimed by Reinhold Niebuhr half a century ago, the doctrine of original sin. It is simply Jesus as Lord. The point at issue is Christological: whether it is the peace *which God has given* that determines the peace which we seek, and which therefore forbids us to fashion for ourselves an unreal goal of ultimate peace which is no more than the projection of unsatisfied human longings.

And so it is that we are invited to pray, in the penultimate petition, to be shown "the peace we must forgo"—the peace which stands next to that horizon of final peace, but which is not that true horizon but a false one. The gateway to a holy love of peace is the refusal of an unholy peace, which attracts us precisely because it offers to legitimate unholy aspirations. Christian love of peace must be purged by the refusal of this peace.[11] On this point, if I judge him rightly, the true Christian pacifist is in agreement. He understands that his witness to peace must be modelled upon the sacrifice of Christ upon the cross. He knows that the peace of the Kingdom of Heaven is won only by the costly refusal of substitutes. But, as Professor Anscombe once wrote, "pacifism has corrupted enormous numbers of people who will not act according to its tenets."[12] She had in mind especially those who learn from pacifists to deny the moral difference between slaying the innocent and slaying the guilty;

11. Matthew 10:34, pll. Luke 12:51.
12. G. E. M. Anscombe, "War and Murder", in *Nuclear Weapons and Christian Conscience,* ed. Walter Stein (Merlin, 1961), p. 56.

but the point can be taken more widely. Simple love of peace is corrupting when it is not accompanied by a readiness to sacrifice the peace which pretends to be what it is not. That, as it stands, is not a criticism of Christian pacifism but of its sentimental imitations. A war-weary civilisation, eager to secure the goal of peace on terms that will cost no more bloodshed, dreams of an evolving historical necessity which will bring peace once and for all, and lays impatient claim on the world-transforming powers of technology in order to conjure that peace into existence. The moral *askesis* that such a civilisation needs is to turn away from the pursuit of peace and to attend to its responsibility for justice. Any quest for peace that is not linked to a quest for justice will be illusory.

But, of course, the promotion of justice, too, demands of us the same refusal of false ultimates. Final justice is not to be looked for, any more than final peace is to be looked for, until they are both shown to us in the face of Jesus Christ. Humane judgment is necessarily a more restricted affair than that divine judgment for which we hope. It must strike a balance with the possible; otherwise it becomes a community-destroying fanaticism. This, I suppose, is the message of that most deeply Christian work of art, Shakespeare's *Merchant of Venice*.

When we try to determine the extent of the justice that is possible for us to realise in international affairs, we raise again, and this time correctly, the question of peace, "the peace we can keep". Such peace as can be kept and such justice as is defended in keeping it define and limit each other. We may not say that we will

never go to war for justice's sake; but neither may we
say that we will never accept a compromise of justice
for the sake of peace. The pursuit of this relative peace
is always the character of well-judged political prudence, even when we practice the necessary ascetic discipline of postponing questions of peace to questions
of justice. "Even wars are waged with peace as their
goal."[13] So if we say that the problem with deterrence
is that it makes just wars too difficult to fight, we must
add by way of elaboration that it thereby inhibits the
pursuit of a judicious peace, "the peace we can keep".

There is, within this phrase "can keep", the suggestion of divine permission. That is to say: there is a
peace that we *can* keep because we *may* keep it; and
we *may* keep it because God has given us proof of his
will for our social good which may and must shape
our actions. The ultimate is not merely a negation of
the penultimate. Certainly, the fact that God's will is
declared only in the face of Christ *limits* the significance of our actions and negates their pretensions to
ultimacy. Yet at the same time it *shapes* their significance, giving them an importance precisely as a penultimate reflection of the final peace-giving. The pres-
ent-day disciples of Niebuhr can sometimes be
accused of treating the possibilities of the present too
negatively, as a sphere which is not only not the final
peace, but which is not even formed or shaped by the
final peace, a sphere outside the reach of the Incarna-
tion, where original sin alone prevails. They might
learn from St. John of Patmos, who cannot be accused

13. Augustine, *De civitate Dei* XIX.12.1.

of vacuous optimism, that politics in the Christian era is marked by new possibilities: possibilities of demonic idolatry on the one hand and of effective witness to the truth on the other. The great city, in which the two prophets of God daily rebuked evil in the market-place and no one dared harm them, contained possi-bilities enough for political action, even though its possibilities also included the prophets' martyrdom.[14] There is too much resignation in some forms of real-ism, and too little resonance of the Gospel, which in-cludes the promise that our human works are not in vain in the Lord.[15]

"The peace we can keep, the peace we must forgo." Essentially the whole field of political prudence is de-scribed and delimited in these two phrases, and in asking for grace to know them apart we are asking for the sum of political wisdom. Yet there is a further peti-tion, which stands ahead of these two on the middle-ground of human action and renunciation. It belongs to that ground and not to the horizon; and yet it is not a petition for political wisdom strictly understood, but for a wisdom that lies beyond politics, and which shapes and sustains politics. "Show us the peace we may give." New acts of reconciliation, new initiatives to overcome old hostility may not be recommended by a strictly *political* judgment; and yet they may be necessary if the balance of earthly peace, with which the political process concerns itself, is not to degener-ate into perpetual strife. We pray for these possibili-ties, too, possibilities for re-orienting the political dis-

14. Revelation 11:3-6.
15. Cf. 1 Corinthians 15:58.

cussion; that we may not simply keep the peace, but may be able to take initiatives to enhance the peace we keep, and so protect it against entropy.

Two Stages of Disarmament

It is entirely reasonable to think that one of the acts of peace-giving which are needed to sustain and renew the conditions of peace is disarmament—not merely the renunciation of deterrence, that is, but a more far-reaching reduction in the scale of defences. It is a moral duty of every generation to attempt to deflate the language of hostility: to make mild reproof do instead of hard words, to make hard words do instead of small attacks, to make small attacks do instead of large ones, and (especially in a technologically inflationary age) to resist the temptation to let the means available dictate the scale of means used. Our own period of history has not been without its own recognition of this, appalling as the technological engrossment of its weapons has been. The diplomatic and military services have continued to appreciate that anger can be communicated by small symbolic gestures and that controlled, well-judged actions are quite as effective as massive assaults. Such wise traditions as these have lain behind attempts to deflate the scale of nuclear armaments and create a capacity for limited nuclear war.[16] These attempts themselves would have been wise, had their meaning not been

16. We may mention especially President Carter's initiative of 1980, usually referred to by the title of the document,

distorted by the context of deterrence. Certainly, nothing to the point was said against them by opponents of deterrence who thought it sufficient to declaim that nobody could win a limited nuclear war—thus assuming, like any true-believing deterrentist, that we are safest when all our weapons are large ones!

However, the failure of such attempts to introduce the traditional wisdom of deflation into deterrence indicates the distinctiveness of that problem. In the deterrence-context peace cannot be pursued in the traditional way, as though the problem were simply a larger-scale version of the problem that civilisations have always faced. Deterrence is something different from what has always been done. The attempt to introduce the infinite into sanctions is something different from the mere exaggeration of sanctions. Until we have successfully removed the appeal to the infinite, we cannot set about the work of deflation. The giving of peace must, therefore, take form in two stages, of which the first, the renunciatory stage, should proceed unilaterally if it cannot be made to proceed in any other way, and is guided by our need to have a language of hostilities which *could* be used for just and proportionate action. The second stage is to pursue, by multilateral undertaking, a common deflation of the language of hostilities, so that action, when it is necessary, can be taken with less damage and less loss of life than has been the case in most modern wars. Failure to grasp the two-stage character of the peace

---

Presidential Directive 59. See Freedman, *Evolution of Nuclear Strategy,* pp. 392-95.

quest is another sign that we do not know what we are doing when we practise deterrence. Treating all disarmament as a seamless web, urgently hurrying on from talk of nuclear renunciation to the pursuit of further arms-reductions until war (the day after tomorrow, or possibly the next day) shall be no more; all this, forgiveable as it may be, is but another instance of the same greedy thirst for peace without justice which gave rise to the project of deterrence in the first place.[17]

17. Arguably, if the nuclear dimension to our forces were abolished, then the need for stronger conventional forces would be less, since one of the roles they have to play in the present state of affairs is to *prolong the war*, avoiding a quick resolution at the conventional level which would drive either side to nuclear use. Thus the U.S. Catholic bishops (in *The Challenge of Peace*, p. 68) are not entirely misguided in expressing the hope "that a significant reduction in numbers of conventional arms and weaponry would go hand in hand with diminishing reliance on nuclear deterrence." As expressed, however, the hope is hardly well-founded. For, in the first place, a reduction in conventional arms cannot go hand in hand with *diminishing* reliance on nuclear weapons, since only the *total absence* of reliance on nuclear weapons, including those for which a just use might be imagined, could relieve the burden currently laid upon our conventional forces of preventing any conflict from going nuclear. In the second place, since there is no moral reason for a categorical ban on *all* nuclear weapons, there is no *moral* ground for demanding *categorically* that the conditions for a reduction in conventional forces should ever be met. It is reasonable, of course, to allow some weight to the general moral presumption in favor of deflated hostilities. But how and when this presumption is to affect our posture of defense must be a judgment of pru-

In order to contemplate the first stage it is not necessary for anyone to dream dreams of other worlds
than now exist, of worlds, for example, in which nuclear weapons are but a painful memory and in which
the very technique for manufacturing them has either
been forgotten or is locked up under armed guard at
some Headquarters of World Government. The difficulty of imagining such a world is often made the basis
of a fatalist argument—the old technological optimism now turned sour and despairing—that we are
locked into deterrence for ever. But the argument is an
irrelevance. If we are locked into deterrence, it is not
by the existence of technical information and skills,
but by our failure to see that the pursuit of infinite
sanctions is useless to the cause of peace, obstructive
to the tasks of justice, and pretty inconvenient even to
the purposes of self-interest and tyranny. To take a par-
allel case: when terrorists first began hijacking aircraft
by brandishing hand grenades in midflight, did anybody suggest that the answer was to equip pilots and
crew with hand grenades to retaliate with? Or bewail
the fact that we were *locked into* such a response by the
mere fact that hand grenades were readily available to
terrorists? A response which made no sense would always make no sense, whomever the means was avail-

---

dence. The bishops' claim that in expressing this unguarded
hope (while failing to distinguish it in kind from the categorical moral demand which requires the abandonment of the
deterrent, a demand which they have allowed to become un-
duly muffled), they "contribute a moral dimension to the discussion" (*sc* of conventional weapons), verges, I am afraid, on
the sanctimonious.

able to. A programme of meticulous policing of airports, in-flight guards trained to shoot with great accuracy, and international agreements to prosecute has reduced the menace, despite the fact that hand grenades are as accessible as ever. The continued possibility of manufacturing high-yield nuclear weapons, in a world completely disabused of the dogmas of deterrence, would be of no interest to anybody, since nobody would have a use for them; in a world only partially disabused it would be of interest simply from the point of view of policing, a task barely undertaken today.

The first task of disarmament and rearmament, then, is to set an initial ceiling of destructiveness on our armoury, so that it contains only such forces as might be useful in possible conflicts, and to provide a sufficient range of less destructive capabilities to permit effective fighting to proceed with reasonable economy of force. It is then for the second stage to pursue a more general prejudice in favour of minimising destructiveness and exercising a downward pressure on the language of hostilities. That is the context in which we may pursue our proper anxieties about the still horrific character of modern technological warfare even at the conventional or lower nuclear level. Those anxieties, as I say, are entirely proper; but so long as we allow them to dominate the agenda, and so obstruct serious thinking about the first stage, we have failed to realise that in deterrence we have done something different, and worse, than merely making war gross. It is an aesthetic rather than a moral reaction to be ruled by this horror, and it feeds directly back into the sources of the modern yearning for perpetual peace.

So there will be no perpetual peace, short of the day when judgment and reconciliation will be one? Well, strife will not atrophy and die merely because of our loathing for it. It continues to perform an essential, if unrecognised, function as the last resort of justice. "The tygers of wrath are wiser than the horses of instruction", said Blake. We may, however, possibly train the tigers of wrath to *become* horses of instruction to this limited extent: we may devise more effective institutions than now exist for the administration of justice between nations, institutions which will, of course, be neither perfectly just nor perfectly authoritative, but may carry a sufficient degree of credibility both in the quality of their judgments and in the effectiveness of their power to command. But even so, these horses of instruction will need to carry with them the wisdom they had as tigers. They will not introduce the reign of peace and goodwill, but merely a new disposition of the same elements of political action: coercion limited and directed by judgment. The best that we can hope for is to build upon the legacy of international law some forms of effective international sanction. Failing that, we must be content to hope for a scaling down of the means of war and for a strengthening of those laws of war which protect non-combatants from direct attack. Even of this more modest goal we may perhaps have to say, as the great Grotius said of the ever-elusive unity of the Christian churches: "Well, yet it is a contentment to be and to live and to die in the wishes of so great a good." But

we can mean exactly what we say. There need be no
shadow of resignation to darken our contentment; for
our labours of peace-keeping and peace-giving are not
in vain in the Lord.